HAPPINESS IS AN INSIDE JOB

BROKEN BUT NOT BITTER

HAPPINESS

is an

INSIDE JOB

BROKEN
BUT NOT BITTER

ARLISIA STALEY

Happiness Is An Inside Job – Broken But Not Bitter
For speaking engagements, contact Arlisia Staley at:
True Sisterhood Women's & Leaders Fellowship
16333 Green Tree Blvd., #2184
Victorville, CA 92395
truesisterhood4god@gmail.com

ISBN: 978173440630

Scriptures marked NIV are taken from the NEW INTERNATIONAL VERSION (NIV): Scripture taken from THE HOLY BIBLE, NEW INTERNATIONAL VERSION ®. Copyright© 1973, 1978, 1984, 2011 by Biblica, Inc.™. Used by permission of Zondervan

Scriptures marked NLT are taken from the HOLY BIBLE, NEW LIVING TRANSLATION (NLT): Scriptures taken from the HOLY BIBLE, NEW LIVING TRANSLATION, Copyright© 1996, 2004, 2007 by Tyndale House Foundation. Used by permission of Tyndale House Publishers, Inc., Carol Stream, Illinois 60188. All rights reserved. Used by permission.

Scriptures marked KJV are taken from the KING JAMES VERSION (KJV): KING JAMES VERSION, public domain.

Book cover design by Tanja Prokop
Book formatting by Graciela Aničić

First printing edition 2020

Arlisia Staley, Publisher
16333 Green Tree Blvd., #2184
Victorville, California 92395
truesisterhood4god@gmail.com

CONTENTS

DEDICATION

I dedicate this book to the memory of my AMAZING parents Mr. Wilson & Ms. Josephine, who were married for sixty-four years. They truly loved me and were the best parents God could have entrusted me to. As a child,I thought they were just too strict, but now I see it as pure wisdom and love. I appreciate them for teaching me, instructing me and telling me *no* when I wanted to hear *yes*. Their no protected me. I'm thankful that they restricted the number of times I spent overnight at my friends' homes, though I didn't understand it at the time. When they put constraints on me, it was actually God in action. My dad worked and took care of our home, made sure we never went without food, clothing and life's necessities. If my mom was reading this, she would look at me and say, "I don't know what you're talking about--there was a time I worked two jobs." My mother was a licensed daycare mother. I like to explain her job this way: she helped raise other people's children, treating them like family, while their parents went to work.They listened to and followed my mother's instructions. She didn't just watch them, she raised them with tender love. A gentleman whose son my mom took care of, reached out to me today and sent these words of endearment about my parents; "I know your mother had a powerful impact on this world, and so did your father. They were the Sanford and Son king and queen (they both loved watching Sanford & Son). I can still smell the cornbread that was baking when I picked up my son. I have great, loving memories of them. They were a blessing to me." His son is now in his 30's. His kind words are appreciated. My heart overflows with gratitude for their dedication to parenting and being amazing people. I still live by the words she consistently drilled in me, "It's nice to be nice. You reap what you sow. If you don't have nothing nice to say, don't say nothing at all. Treat people the way you desire to be treated. Why buy the cow when the milk is free? "They are both truly missed. Eternally grateful, your baby girl.

ACKNOWLEDGEMENTS

Dr. Dee Dee Freeman, I would like to express my deepest appreciation for your time and concern during this trying season. Your expression of love will never be forgotten. Your thoughtfulness is a gift I will always treasure.

Evangelist Leighla Rolland, thank you. You didn't know my name, but you allowed Holy Spirit to minister and strengthen me for the battle. I am undoubtedly changed beyond words. Bless you for your instinctive obedience, which is a principal character I truly admire. Such was glorious days when you encouraged me at noon day prayer, during those hot Summer months. God's glory was tangible. His divine presences sufficiently met us each and every day. That's what I call a real hot girl summer, when you can pray heaven down with no air conditioner. I shall remember this season for a lifetime. God is faithful! I am so blessed.

Sgt. Jeff Monroe, I am beyond appreciative you were the officer dispatched at 12:16 AM September 4, 2017, early Monday morning, shortly before my beloved mother took her final breath. The official San Bernardino County Sheriff Departments' motto is "Dedicated to Your Safety" you superseded the call of duty. In addition, you demonstrated compassion and strength. I did not recognize a uniform; I observed a person who was human. I looked up the word commendable in the modern dictionary, and the definition was: Sgt. Jeff Monroe. In an ideal world September 4th would be SGT. Jeff Monroe's Day.

Evangelist Vickie Harris Trigg, thank you for being the first person to peruse this mandate. You have been my cheerleader and an encouraging voice as I endeavored to complete this act of love. You are a gift. And people who are fortunate to experience your love are blessed.

Last but not least, Pastor Eugene Blount, the words Holy Spirit spoke into my life through you, will live with me throughout my lifetime. Holy Spirit said, "It was not to kill you, but it was to bring you to another level. The enemy would have desired to kill you, but I'm going to use it for my glory. Don't die in the transition Prophetess, Don't die in the transition Prophetess, Don't die in the transition Prophetess, Don't die in the valley Prophetess, Don't die in the pit Prophetess, because I'm getting ready to bring you out! I'm getting ready to place you in the palace. You've been in the cave I am pulling you out." Woo! Those words encouraged me to my core. Bless you for obeying God and hosting noon day prayer. The POWER of God was great in that storefront building. God specialized in meeting the needs of His people in the prayer services. I feel God orchestrated noon day prayer just for me.

Thank you to everyone who prayed or shared an encouraging word.

I love and appreciate each of you.

PREFACE

At the outset, let me say that I had no intention of ever sharing the things I've written here. But the Lord said, "Don't worry about the opinions of others. I want you to tell your story for the benefit of those who need to know how to get through the tough stuff, and I will be with them every step of the way." If you take nothing else away from this book, hold onto this reassuring truth: God will be with you through every season of your life, no matter how difficult or humiliating, if you invite Him. I never imagined I would be forced to face overwhelming challenges on several different fronts all at the same time. I'd been caring for my ailing ninety-three-year old mother for four years, when my husband suddenly abandoned me without any warning, to deal with things alone.

It looked like the enemy was in control, but it was actually a season of death, burial, and resurrection as it related to that time of my life. I will experience more deaths as I endeavor to be more like Him, Daddy Abba. It was my character-building season. When I say God strengthened and comforted me through this uncomfortable season, there are no words to explain the magnitude of His comfort. It blew me away how He stood between me, the blows and the pain. I am so thankful!

God was with me when I had come to the end of my strength and had no other choice but to give my mother twenty-four-hour care until the end, after she could no longer care for herself. He covered me with His wings and stayed with me, when endless attacks were launched, and even tried to kill me. I was astonished and inordinately blessed when He stood between me, the blows and the pain, and graciously provided finances, natural strength and mental stability that was so badly needed when I was at my lowest.

Isaiah 43:2 NIV tells us: "When you go through the deep waters, I will be with you. When you go through the rivers of difficulty, you will not drown; When you walk through the fire of oppression, you will not be burned; the flames will not consume you." If you're facing insurmountable issues, tempted to lose hope and throw in the towel, repeat this scripture aloud, and get it in your spirit, because it will comfort and encourage you to know that you're not alone; He is sending angels to fight your battles for you and bring you through victorious.

Not long ago I met four college students from out of state in Los Angeles, CA. UCLA was hosting an event in which they were competing. During our conversation we began discussing relationships, and when I told them I was writing a book on the subject, they expressed great interest. When they asked the name of the book, I had to admit that I hadn't yet decided on a title. Just before they left, I said, "Happiness is an inside job." One of the students said, "Hey, that's a perfect title for your book!" In that instant, I knew she was right. Hence the title *Happiness is an Inside Job*, which it truly is.

In the beginning I found it a challenge to write. In fact, I would sometimes experience chest pains, and other days the process seemed exceedingly draining, which meant that, in the end, it took far longer to complete it. But praise God, who is always faithful, to help us finish what we begin.

MY OWN POINT OF REFERENCE

Before I married my husband, I could see issues—he was clearly spoiled by his mother. It was clear to me that, he was the person they depended on to keep them company, fix and repair things around the house, etc. It's also important for you to know that, before we married, I was not looking for a mate or even eager to marry. I was not desperate to be married. As a matter of fact, I had often enjoyed going alone, to dinner, concerts or movies. But I was eager to live in the center of God's will, so I asked Him to show me what to do, and I followed His leading. He made it clear and confirmed it several times that this man was the one for me, and I had to trust that He knew what He was doing, no matter what it looked like in the natural. After we married, it wasn't long before the generational curses began to manifest, as he tried to control me, withheld access to our jointly-held finances, and refused to add my name to our bank accounts. However, he would soon learn that I was not a pushover nor did I tolerate injustice. I often stood up to him and refused to back down regarding the right thing to do.

*Grace alert. It was God's grace that brought me through the season when my husband decided to walk away from God. Going into that time, I was aware that I had been called to marry this man. And though it wasn't an easy time, I knew that if God had anointed me for such a time as this, He would also be faithful to protect and provide for me, and He never once failed me.

I would *never* recommend marrying unless God confirms His will and you know, know, know, that it's God, and not just your own questionable choice. You cannot walk through what I went through and come out unscathed without God's clear anointing and calling. My 'yes' was simply an act of my worship, in obedience to my Father.

Some may say that God wouldn't call you into such a marriage. I would have to reply by saying that God doesn't call those who aren't willing to obey what He says, no matter the cost. In fact, God said: "I'm going to use you in this place, but there will be no reference point. You'll have to seek Me for instructions." On 4/19/17, God said this: "I'm using your life to show others that I am God. People have put Me in a box, trying to limit what I do, because one person says it is so, and they believe it. They don't have the testimony for themselves. I am God. I turn the hearts of men whichever way I choose. Too many have walked away from *miracles, based on hearsay, not a proven method.* Daughter, you cannot fulfill My heart's desire, and I not fulfill yours. Watch me flex My muscles."

In Hosea 1:2 we find that God told Hosea to marry a prostitute named Gomer. In the New Testament we read that the Apostle Paul was transformed, from one who persecuted the saints, into a great example of an evangelist who was ultimately beheaded for the gospel. From those two examples, we can see that God sometimes does things His way just to show He can--things that don't make sense in the natural. All I did was marry a man God wanted to bring out of a dark place. In the end, we must agree that God's ways are not our ways nor His thoughts our thoughts. (Isaiah 55:8.)

CHAPTER 1

Fantasy vs reality

CHAPTER 1

Fantasy vs reality

At some point, long after you've said, "I do," --long after the ceremony is over, and memories are all that linger of that wonderful day, this chapter will resonate with you.

Marriage is about much more than wanting someone to share your life because you're lonely. Ask those in divorce court who can't wait to sit in a room without the partner they once couldn't live without. It's far more than needing someone to accompany you to dinner parties, have children with, to attend church with, or as a travel companion. None of those reasons have kept people out of divorce court.

Marriage is a ministry. Just as Christ went through death, burial, and resurrection so you could live, you and your marriage must evolve, under the direction of the Holy Spirit, as you become more like Christ. Jeremiah 29:11 NIV reads: "For I know the plans I have for you, says the Lord, plans to prosper you and not to harm you, plans to give you a hope and a future." But that hope and future must align with God's original design for our lives, in the same way Christ loved His bride.

Someday the time will come when you look at your spouse, even just for a second, and say, "Will someone please remind me why I gave up the single life? Who signed me up for this?" Allow me to answer you in advance—you did, now do the work! *The truth is that marriage is a full-time job and you cannot call in sick!* Marriage will use muscles you didn't know you had-- mentally, emotionally, and verbally. As a matter of fact, you will, no doubt, have to develop special muscles just for that purpose.

Marriage is a covenant relationship you enter with your husband, before God and witnesses. During that auspicious occasion the minister asks a series of questions, to which you answer and vow before God, by saying "I do." And whether anyone else believes it or not, God takes those vows very seriously, expecting us to honor our promises to be faithful until death do us part. In order to keep those all-important marriage vows, you must first understand the concept of covenant and the seriousness of the vows you're making. In scripture, we find that God made a covenant with Abraham, promising that if His people would serve Him with all their hearts, souls and minds, He would bless them in the city, in the country, and in everything they did as long as they lived. The man you desire to marry must also esteem the covenant as a one and done event, that will have no end as long as you live. When a husband and wife agree to please God by keeping the covenant they made when they said "I do" they can work through any situation together.

God never intended for a covenant to be broken. A covenant is till death do you part.

Divorce is the result of a submission problem, a heart issue, or a pride issue before God, and actually has little or nothing to do with your spouse. Obedience takes strength; submission takes strength. If you fail to grow in your willingness to obey, you'll be devastated when the future of your relationship requires it. You can't afford to live in disappointment, because in the end, it will rob you of time, strength and concentration. Resolve now to do whatever it takes to make it through to the end.

Samuel had become emotionally attached to Saul's future, so he was deeply grieved when Saul walked away from God, but God responded with a command to get up and stop grieving. In other words, God was saying that we as His people, are to do everything as a sacrifice of praise unto the Lord. Even in marriage when your spouse is having a bad day or a difficult season, love him as unto the Lord. The reward will be worth it.

Marriage is not for the faint at heart, rookies, crybabies, mama's boys, or I-can-do-no-wrong daddy's girls. Marriage was instituted by God, and stamped with this singular phrase: "So they are no longer two, but one flesh. Therefore, what I have joined together let no man put asunder" (Matthew 19:6). Asunder means to break apart or in two, or to become parted or severed.

Believe me when I say that you can expect hell to come against what God has joined together, and the enemy will use family, friends or foes and even us as individuals, to undermine our relationships. This is one of the many reasons you must come into marriage not only spiritually equipped, but also healed, delivered and set free from generational family issues, ungodly influences, and your own tendencies to be counterproductive.

So often people go into relationships and marriage, expecting someone else to make them happy. If you go into a marriage for that reason, your marriage could implode, because no one but you, can actually make you happy. As you've no doubt heard before, happiness is a choice--an inside job," it would remove the stress if you settled the issue before you get married. If you're already married, you can take the strain off your marriage by seeking counseling, becoming whole, because that's what agape love is all about—preferring others rather than demanding our own way. Isn't that the love Christ exemplified toward us?

The truth is that some people are perpetually unhappy, because of issues from their past. Why would you want to give anyone that much power over you? The moment they're un-happy, there goes your happiness. It's far too burdensome to live like that, and above all, it's not God's plan for marriage. If you marry a man so you can be happy, wouldn't it be heartbreaking to discover that he himself is miserable, fighting childhood issues of abuse, anger, or betrayal? If you're hoping to marry, ask God to sharpen your discernment—your spiritual vision. Refuse to put on blinders, and do not turn a deaf ear to the reality of what Holy Spirit will reveal regarding a potential spouse. Just because he has positive traits you admire, doesn't mean he's God's choice of a mate for you.

It could mean that it's a season for you to fast and pray for his healing or deliverance, in order to destroy any satanic strongholds in his life.Matthew 17:21 NIV reads: "But this kind does not go out except by prayer and fasting." If this describes your situation, allow it to come about as a result of Holy Spirit leading, and not of your own choosing. I don't believe love is blind; I do believe there are times women would rather not know and hear the truth, in fear of losing a relationship, but that leaves them in the darkness to their great misfortune.

I want to caution you not to rush into marriage no matter what! Does that mean you have a license to sleep around because you're burning with lust? Absolutely not! I talk to men who have said time and time again, "God knows my needs, and I know He will make exception for me, because He knows my heart." My answer, God doesn't change His Word to fit your needs. Hear God, pray, find out if your intended is the person God has for you. If he or she is the one, you must seek God for His timing. Do not allow anyone or anything, including your need for sex, your biological clock, or family pressure to cause you to move ahead of God! This could be a season of preparation. But absolutely do **not** marry out of desperation, because you and your heart will pay a hefty price for it. And if God says not to marry that person, **obey Him**, remembering that just as obedience reaps a harvest, so does disobedience. Trust me, it's a harvest you do not want to reap. Philippians 4:6-7 tells us: "Do not be anxious about anything, but by prayer and petition, with thanksgiving, present your requests to God. And the peace of God, which transcends all understanding, will guard your hearts and your minds in Christ Jesus."

Ladies, ask questions

When women tell me that a man has expressed interest and is asking questions to get to know them better, I ask them if they are asking questions. I'm always astonished when they say they know nothing and haven't asked any questions. What? How does that happen? How is it that they've revealed everything about themselves, then quickly become smitten with someone they know nothing about!

If you want to marry, it's imperative to ask important questions when you meet a man who is interested in getting to know you. See if you're even on the same page. Ladies, you must stop worrying about scaring off a man, if you ask questions. In fact, you should rejoice and be exceedingly glad if that makes him back off enough to go away. The harsh truth is that you will settle for anyone, if you marry simply because you're afraid of growing old alone. As my mother used to say, don't just settle for a pair of pants. Men have no problem asking questions, and neither should women who are wise. All questions can be asked with respect, in a matter-of-fact way.

Here are a few telling questions you can ask at the outset. Don't wait until you've dated for a while, or once you start to fall in love. If you wait until you're smitten, your feelings will take the lead over the logic and Holy Spirit leading in your spirit. You'll tell yourself that he's

nice and has a decent job; he calls and seems attentive —
and you will settle. Here are a few sample questions:

1. Who is Jesus to you? If he doesn't let you know
   in no uncertain terms that Jesus is Lord of his
   life. What if you find he doesn't believe in Jesus?
   Will you step away immediately, because you
   don't want to settle for being unequally yoked
   with an unbeliever, or do you?

2. Do you attend Bible Study? You want to know--
   is he being challenged to grow? Does he submit
   to leadership? You also want to know if he has a
   teachable spirit.

3. What are your long and short-term goals? You
   want to know if he has a plan. If not, how can
   you be supportive of his plan? God created you
   to be a help-mate. How is he going to lead and
   cover you?

4. What are your interests? He might be a couch
   potato and unmotivated, expecting you to
   support him.

5. Are you married? He can't say you didn't ask.

6. Have you ever been married?

7. How many times have you been married?

8. Do you presently live alone or with someone?
   Have you ever lived with anyone who wasn't
   your spouse?(If he has a roommate ask whether
   that person is male or female. If female, did
   the two of you once date?Are they currently
   sleeping together?)

9. Do you have children? (Ladies if you marry a man and you don't want him to discipline your child/children from a previous relationship, that's going to be a problem in your marriage.)

10. Do you want children?If you want children and he doesn't, don't waste time developing a relationship, because you'll only be hurt and resentful later. Do you have time to waste?

11. What is your perspective on finances and debt? This is a very important topic. Does he spend more than he makes? It takes finances to live. You also need to know if he's reasonably generous, or miserly, pinching every penny. He could be in so much debt from a previous divorce that he can barely make ends meet without your support. I've personally heard men say they need to get a girlfriend to live with, for financial assistance.

The importance of asking questions is to obtain information in the beginning. Otherwise, you might end up saying, "I didn't know that about you." Well, did you ask?

Use wisdom if you decide to ask the following questions. You will know the appropriate time to ask them. The following questions are sample questions only:

1. What method of discipline would you use on a child? It can become a problem if one believes

in using a stick (abuse) to spank and the other believes in time-outs or no discipline at all.

2. If you have children, would you mind if I corrected them? If this is a problem, your marriage may end in resentment and ultimately, in divorce, which is not uncommon.

3. Are you paying child support? If yes, are you up to date on your payments?

4. From your perspective, what is a woman's role in marriage?

5. Do you want your wife to work while raising the children? How would you feel if she prefers to work?

6. How do you define the word 'intimacy' (as opposed to sex)?

7. Would you consider your wife as an equal partner in marriage?

Girl, I could go on, but the point here is this: refuse to be desperate enough to walk blindly into a relationship, without discovering the answers to basic questions you dare not ignore. Men will often ask fifty different questions while we women sit there at dinner, too shy to eat, sipping water while trying to look cute. Ask me how I know? I use to be that person when I was younger. You want someone who wants you. You want someone you don't have to chase. You want your future husband to be someone who's committed for the long haul, no matter what. He is not your son, so step out of the mother role, convinced that you are more than enough and you deserve to be loved. Get your emotions under control, and take your heart off your sleeve. Take the process very seriously. You need to have all the facts and act upon them, eliminating anyone who doesn't meet the qualifications of a committed man, who loves Jesus first and foremost, mature and broken before the Lord.

Stop, look, listen, follow through, and wait on God. Refuse to be quick to fall in love. The reality is that we don't actually, *fall* in love. We grow in love. When we are mature, we make a conscious decision to be in love and commit to loving someone. Stay alert, and be clear about what you see. Refuse to put on blinders. Don't let your emotions run your life, or dictate your choices, because emotions often lie to us, though we may not realize it until we've gone too far to change our minds. My mother used to say, "Don't have diarrhea of the mouth." Become a great listener and listen for what you need to hear. Be a conscientious observer, and look for the follow-through along with consistency. Fake can't continue to be fake for long. Remember that old saying that talk is cheap? Apply it to this area of your life. Let me repeat: Stop, look, listen, follow through, and wait on God.

I keep reiterating myself because I know a lot of women have the desire to be married, and that's awesome. I also know how excited they get when a man decides to say "hello." Did you know a man can sense when you are naive, desperate, or confident?

You want to give yourself enough time to find out who the person really is before you commit. Do not be desperate! Don't relinquish to another, your most precious possessions--your mind and heart, before you find out who he really is, where he is going in life, and the most importantly, whether or not he's God's man for you.Notice that I didn't mention your body among your most precious possessions? Save that for your wedding night. No ringy, no dingy until after you say, "I Do." You can't fall in love, give yourself completely, including your body, then cry foul when the fantasy in your head doesn't work out the way you were hoping. And why didn't it work out? Because it was a fantasy. Real relationships leading to marriage demand dedicated, consistent work from both individuals, who are passionate and committed to each other. If he's not excited about you, he's not the one.

It's difficult when dating to understand exactly what marriage entails, before you say 'I Do." Can you discern the challenges that lie ahead? While you're dating, you aren't dealing with the responsibility of bills, decisions, kids and the other details involved in a marriage relationship. You're not dealing with how the other person was raised. There are men who would rather date and remain unmarried. There is no responsibility involved, no commitment no stress.

You deserve God's best, wait for a man who is serious about love, and willing to take responsibility for a wife and family. Wait for true love. I hope you will not settle for anything less than the whole package. Too many ladies settle for lust, which benefits self at the expense of others. Love means serving your spouse, while lust will use whoever it must to fulfill its selfish desires.

Don't fall in love with love, and settle for less than the real thing. I was watching a show on television, I was astounded at how many people fall for online catfish scammers, who fake an online profile and fake friends, putting up fake photos and pretending to be someone they aren't. Sometimes they scam more than one person at a time, even perfect strangers--out of jealousy, revenge, greed or loneliness. Some have been known to sit in a cubicle and send out multiple phone numbers, so they can identify the caller by the number they dial. The perpetrator will send a photo, claiming that it's them, then back it up with fraudulent pictures of jobs, cities or countries. Note that they will never let you see their real faces by meeting in person, or video chatting. They will almost always share a sad story, in order to get unsuspecting women to give as much money as possible for as long as possible. They will also try to get the victim's bank information, so they can swindle them that way as well. And even after police and private investigators prove the men are frauds and don't actually exist, the women have already fallen in love, and refuse to believe the truth. In reality, they fell in love with the illusion of love, and in the end, were swindled out of hundreds of thousands of dollars they will never get back.

In this day and age, if you date, you need to be savvy, up on your game, and have a keen sense of spiritual discernment, to protect yourself from scammers.

Ladies, beware. Never send money to a man you met over the phone or online, or to anyone you've never met in person, someone you know nothing about. We must stop being naïve and vulnerable, risking what we can't afford to lose. You should not have to buy happiness, because: "Happiness Is an Inside Job." A true gentleman, is a man who is reliable and authentic, and will never ask you for money under any circumstance when you meet. Rather, he will come, sincerely wanting to know how he can serve you--how he can make your life better. I'm heartbroken to see scammers take advantage of ladies-- some of whom are over the age of fifty and widowed or divorced. If this describes you, choose to trust God and refuse to be desperate enough to do anything for what looks like love, but is really a nightmare from which you can't wake up. Take this advice: If he comes asking for money, he isn't the one.

We can't be afraid to let go of what is *not of God*, to obtain what is of God. It's one thing to pray to God, but it's another thing to get up and obey what God has replied in answer to our prayers. In our heads, we may think we're serving God, but in our hearts, we're actually serving our own personal desires.

Proverbs 4:23 says this: – "Above all else, guard your heart, for everything you do flows from it." Guard your emotions and guard your thoughts. When you do, if things go south you won't become bitter and hard, you will have taken responsibility for your own safety and well-being.

It's alarming how women settle for men who they already know are wrong for them. Often, it happens because they're worried that he may be their last chance for a relationship. First off, we need to heed scripture, when it says that fear is torment. Fear causes you to move in a direction away from God. I've seen women who knew a certain man wasn't the one, but instead of asking God for His help to let go, they fought to hold on. Warring against the truth ultimately affected their health, plaguing them with sleepless nights and endless worry. Some would even run from those who dared to tell them the truth, even after asking for their advice. In reality, they didn't want the truth if it was contrary to their desires.

Remember that, in the end you must live with the consequence of your decision that can last months, years, and for some--a lifetime. The wrong relationship can even affect the lives of your children mentally, spiritually, and socially. The wrong decision can hinder or prevent them from living out their destiny. Your children didn't ask to be born; you made a choice that resulted in their births, so make it your priority to protect them at any cost. Even at the cost of a relationship.

Your children deserve your love, protection and attention. My advice? Get as far away as possible from what is not healthy or life-affirming for your children. God isn't obligated to protect us when we step out from under His umbrella of protection. He is only obligated to protect us when we go where He leads. Whether we want to believe it or not, when we go anywhere else in our disobedience, we're fair game for the enemy.

Adam & Eve's disobedience led them away from God's voice to where they could no longer respond to the wooing of God's Spirit. Genesis 3:8-10 reads: "Then the man and his wife heard the voice of the LORD God walking in the garden in the breeze of the day, and they hid themselves from the presence of the LORD God among the trees of the garden. So the LORD God called out to the man, "Where are you?" "I heard Your voice in the garden," he replied, "and I was afraid because I was naked; so I hid."

Surely, for our own best interests and protection, we should want to constantly be moving toward His voice and not away from it.

We often hear that disobedience has consequences. I'm here to tell you from experience that obedience to God's voice, His laws, and instructions are better than any stock market that yields limited dividends. When you move quickly in response to God's instructions, He will reward you beyond anything you could dream or imagine. I'm praying that people begin to see the wisdom of putting God first, in order to discover His best for their lives. God's assignments must come first. We can't drag our feet when it comes to worshipping God, when it was what they were born to do.

The next time you struggle with obeying our loving Father, remember, just as disobedience can have terrible and lasting consequences, obedience has far greater rewards. Disobedience means taking steps away from the answer to your prayer, while obedience leads you one closer to receiving it. Keep moving toward God's voice.

Ask yourself this question: When it comes to a marriage partner, what are your standards? What are your deal breakers? Please don't have a shallow list: He have to be six-one or taller, he must like living by the water, he must like chick flicks, he must have swag, he must know how to dress, he must wear bomb shoes, and have large hands. Do such things really matter in the grand scheme of things?

What about this all-important criteria: He must be willing to wait until marriage, for sex. And if he passionately loves God, he won't want to break His heart by having premarital sex, nor will he ever be in danger of committing adultery, breaking both God's heart and yours.

Loneliness doesn't have to cause you to settle and leap without counting the cost. If you have to buy a man, by paying: the rent/mortgage, the car note for the car he drives, for his gas and giving him lunch money, for his clothes, the kid's clothes, and the babysitter, it's not God's best for you. Some women take men and put them in the script, but that story won't have the happy ending you're hoping for. Did you sense in your heart he wasn't the one? You were only hoping it wasn't so. It's going to be hard to take the fantasy from your head and make it a reality. Happiness must be an inside job, so learn to be content to be yourself, without having to pay to have a man in your life. This is not God's order. Do not be driven by insecurity. You are more than enough! Allow God's love to fill you up with nothing but goodness.

Proverbs 3:5-6 tells us, "Trust in the Lord with all your heart and lean not on your own understanding; in all your ways submit to him, and he will make your paths straight." True worship means acknowledging and then obeying God. On the other hand, you can pray, hear God, and refuse to obey His instructions. Please know that God wants what is best for you. Don't compare or compete with someone else's season. If He says no, you don't need to know why. Just let His no be your no. He can't protect you if you refuse to consult Him and then follow His leading.

Obeying God's instructions is a choice. Not everyone will obey the sound instruction they hear, see, know, and even witness. There is an old saying, "Bought sense is better than told." This saying is so far from true! That's why it's old and played out. Why pay a high price to learn something for yourself when you can learn from someone else's hard-won experience? Listening and learning can save you years of heartache and misery.

Did you know that men aren't the only ones paying child and spousal support? Depending on how many years you are married if you divorce, you may be required to pay, not just emotionally but monetarily, for the remainder of your life or until he gets married again. If you marry a man and you make more money than he does, it's quite likely that you'll be required to pay to maintain the lifestyle to which he's accustomed, whether you like it or not. Count the cost--talk to an attorney if you don't believe me. You may be required to pay child support and or alimony bi-weekly or monthly to a man who has divorced you. Either way, you'll pay emotionally and financially, and if you have children, they too, may end up paying for your willful choices. I aim is to save you from making a painful mistake.

Divorce is not something you want to face. If you know this is not the man for you, then save yourself a great deal of emotional pain and heartache and walk away now. Divorce is a costly process in every way, painful, and degrading. Some people even lose their hair and their minds in the process. Some end up bitter for life. Nobody wins in divorce. It's not worth the hell for a pipe dream.

I was reading about a divorcee who was forced to pay emergency spousal support to her soon-to-be ex-husband. According to one news source she paid $235,000 retroactive spousal support and legal fees, and when he requested $129,000 per month he was granted $29,000 a month until they could settle their legal battles. Ouch, that hurts, but it's a reality.

You want someone who demonstrates faithfulness in both word and deed—someone who is broken, and values covenant marriage, and who loves and honors you and God above all else—these things are priceless.

Now there are some men who love God, but haven't yet been healed from their past issues. Some are poor communicators, while others are selfish, or lack sensitivity or leadership skills. Do you get my point? I am not bashing men who are God's glory, and made in the image of God. However, I want to paint a clear picture: loving God is not enough. Perhaps he can take care of the church but has no idea how to be a spouse. The ideal is to have a man who is balanced in the things of God and one who desires to be healed of his issues and break out of selfishness in order to take care of the needs of his wife and family. Those things are priceless.

DISCLAIMER:

Marriage is not for the faint-of-heart or little leaguers. This is a big-girl game. When you are unready for marriage, you say such things as, "I'm not changing for nobody! Don't nobody tell me what to do!" Marriage will be difficult if you run from confrontation and or communication.

You're unprepared for marriage if you've failed to ask the important questions. For example, "Do you want children?" What if your husband has had a vasectomy and two years later, when you're ready to have a family, he suddenly admits, "Oh dear. Sorry, honey, but I forgot to mention I had a vasectomy a couple of years ago." It clearly won't go over well, and in the end, it could even lead to divorce court. That's how vital it is to have conversations that clear the air, on such important details. Without them, you're walking into a covenant situation blind, and with your hands tied behind your back.

Not long ago, I heard a true story about a man who actually went into marriage without telling his wife he'd had a vasectomy. He allowed her to believe they were trying to have a child, never admitting his dirty secret. I was horrified at his deception, because his wife was at a great disadvantage. Before you marry, it's essential to have a serious prayer life, because God can expose those kinds of secrets, letting you know he isn't the one, before you make a commitment that will be difficult and painful to escape.

Many women have found themselves emotionally attached before knowing the one to whom they've attached themselves. The Bible says to write the vision and make it plain. (Habakkuk 2:2). Space has been provided after each chapter for you to answer clarity questions.When a man starts to pursue you, you can refer back to the your oath to remind yourself not to fall for what is not of God. You must be intentional when making a lifelong covenant commitment. Also, to see yourself and discover the areas in which you have grown.

THE OATH

Write five statements stating what you will not do against God, or yourself when the man God has promised you, walks into your life. Once you've completed it, you'll date it and sign it with your signature. Then find an accountability partner, someone who will hold you accountable, read it to them and have the person to sign it as your witness. Come back and read it periodically until you say "I do."

For example:

1. I will not sacrifice my relationship with God in exchange for sex before marriage.
2. I will not abandon my children to have a relationship.
3. I will not allow myself, out of loneliness, to settle for a relationship which is not God's purpose for my life. I WILL WAIT!
4. I will not entertain a relationship that devalues me as a person or as a woman.

MY OATH BEFORE GOD:

1.

2.

3.

4.

5.

Signed By: _____ Date: _____

Witness' Signature: _____ Date: _____

CLARITY QUESTIONS

In order to line up with God's plan for your life, it's vital to be in sync with His Spirit and living in obedience to His Word.

This segment of the book is to help you focus on you. Clarity questions will allow you to open your eyes to areas you may not normally focus on. Areas that need your attention—to see if you have unresolved needs to pray about. The questions for married ladies will differ from the singles. This is a safe place to take off the mask and be real. You will not be sending your representative when God sends the man He has purposed for your life. You will send the person who has done their work from the inside out. Because "Happiness Is an Inside Job."

I've heard people say, I ain't changing for no body, they must take me as I am!

1. Are you ready and willing to change and adjust your life to be married?

2. What are you not willing to adjust or change to be married? Example: hanging out with your girls, not knowing how to cook, etc.

3. Do you pray for your spouse even when you are upset with him?

Personal reflections

CHAPTER 2

Developing a prayer life

CHAPTER 2

Developing a prayer life

You'll need to stay in constant touch with God, through prayer and Bible study, listening for His instructions, in order to win your battles. If you don't know your God-given rights and inheritance, the enemy will trick you into accepting half-truths and lies, at a price you won't want to pay. Remember, there is nothing good in him; in fact, his goal is to steal, kill and destroy both you and your God-ordained destiny. That's basic 101 teaching; My purpose is to give you a rich and satisfying life. (John 10:10, ESV)

Our experiences should help us become wiser, to move us forward, and cause us to make better decisions. But they should never cripple us, or cause us to walk in fear.

After marrying my husband, I was introduced to a way of life that was completely foreign to me, both mentally and emotionally. He was living in the past, crippled by negative life experiences. Since I was his third wife, he was well-acquainted with the court system. Although we had counseling and conversations and agreed that he should add me to the household bank account, I later discovered that he actually had no intention of putting my name on the bank account or any of his accounts. I later found out this was a family practice. Then things became more complicated because I had a car note with approximately one year left, but I now lived over 100 miles away from where I had done business, and he was reluctant to help me pay my car note and insurance, nor could I pay them because my name wasn't on the household account. When I had only two car payments left, I learned that, he had defaulted on my last two car payments because he didn't want to see my car paid off. He had paid off thousands of dollars of his own debt. In fact, I was infuriated that he'd even paid off thousands and thousands of dollars of debts, including some from his past divorce, with our money, but he objected to paying my last two car notes. He believed that he should be allowed to make the rules and that I should follow them, but that was a problem, because they were completely unreasonable, and unfair.

He had a deep need to control that he inherited from his parents, on top of negative experiences from his childhood. I was not okay with his decision to keep household info from me—his wife. I asked what I would do if something happened to him and I had no way to access our funds, and, after five and a half years, he finally agreed to add my name to the accounts, but in the end, it turned out he had only given me access to our savings account, which held less than $100. In response, while he was out of town, I withdrew the $100 and had a check sent to the house, since the bank was out of town.

Early on, he had argued, using every excuse why he didn't want a joint account at a local bank. I received the check but it came only in his name. I placed it on my desk and said nothing to him. One evening I was away and he went looking on my desk and found the check and signed it and deposited it back into his account then returned it to the envelope on my desk. I thought oh, nice, he signed it. I deposited the check into my account. The check came back returned--it bounced. I didn't know that he had deposited the check back into his account without telling me. I shouldn't have been surprised, because he rarely communicated about anything. The only reason he had that account was that his tax person said we would get several thousand back if we filed jointly. Only then did he finally agree and open a joint account at Chase Bank.

The enemy wants to use your words to gain leverage into your marriage. You can know the Word of God, and have faith, but if you don't show up for the fight, it's over, and he wins. The enemy doesn't want you to fight for your spouse, but against him. That's why he fuels your anger, getting you upset and offended so you can quote what hell is saying about him and agree with hell as it pertains to your spouse. You have now given the enemy, who hates marriage between one man and one woman, permission to come in and take residency through your words. Proverbs 18:21 AMP: "Death and life are in the tongue, And those who love it and indulge it will eat its fruit and bear the consequences of their words."

There have been plenty of times I used my mouth to open the door against my spouse. I had to choose to stop taking his actions personally—stop taking offense. It was difficult, because he was so angry, controlling, and unforgiving, as if he didn't need to be forgiven. What's the saying? "He was a cold piece of work." And he knew it. In fact, he said those exact words himself. He kept a tally of my shortcomings and mistakes; I could do nothing to earn his praise. I was like a scientist, searching for ways to please him. The person you marry must come into the marriage with their own happiness. PERIOD.

It wasn't long before I realized that I could only make him happy if I did it from the inside, motivated by the Spirit. I'd already done everything in my power to make him happy, yet he always magnified my mistakes and offenses. I enjoyed being a wife, shopping for his clothes, cooking his dinner from scratch (I enjoyed doing all of such acts of kindness for him) to take to work, dessert included. His co-workers noticed the dinners he brought to work and they complained when comparing his food to their own modest meals. I could never understand how he was more comfortable with strife than with peace in our home. In fact, when things were peaceful, he would purposely stir up chaos, because his inner man was devoid of peace and in turmoil. There were days I wanted to pay the devil to replace him, reminded of lyrics from a song by Hall & Oates. I was treading in unfamiliar territory, feeling as if God had played a bad joke on me.

At that point, it was very important that I clearly hear from God. I already knew without a doubt, that it had been His will to marry him, so I knew that what He initiated, He would also provide for, and complete.

That meant He would see me through, and I hung onto that promise for dear life. But now it was time for me to choose to let my experience make me better, not bitter, so by submitting myself to the Holy Spirit, that's exactly what I did. And now, I can reach out and strengthen others going through similar challenges. And what's more, when God walks you through a trial, He will let you know *when it's over!* Don't allow the beliefs of others to cause you to miss out the anointing you will receive once you emerge from what God called you to do. During this process, God said, "This is the price you paid for the anointing."

1 Peter 5:10 tells us: "In His kindness God called you to share in his eternal glory by means of Christ Jesus. So after you suffered a little while, He will restore, support, and strengthen you, and He will place you on a firm foundation."

As hard as it was, that trial produced growth in me. Did God intend to kill me, by allowing me to go through all the mental and physical hell I went through? It felt like it at the time. But in the end, God knew I would be changed, and many lives would be touched through my testimony so that He would get the glory. Isn't that what He said to Moses? "Yet I will harden the hearts of the Egyptians, and they will follow the Israelites into the sea. Then I will receive great glory at the expense of Pharaoh and his armies, chariots, and charioteers. When I am finished with Pharaoh and his army, all Egypt will know that I am the Lord!" (Exodus 14:17-18 NIV)

My husband's behavior was modeled by his father--a womanizer who hid finances from his wives. While married, he was simultaneously having children by another woman. All the children ended up being raised in the same house together. My mother-in-law was controlling and could lie to me as easily as she poured a cup of morning coffee.

When my father-in-law passed, he had bank accounts and out-of-town property his present wife knew nothing about. As a matter of fact, a couple of months before his death, she got power of attorney to handle his affairs, which should've been *their* affairs all the years they were married. He had given the information to one of his children to hide many years earlier, but by then, she too had passed away. Some of the property was in her name even after her death. Right before he passed, one of his children brought what was left in his name, to California and gave it to his wife. If it had been me and my dad in that situation claiming to be a Christian, I would've challenged him, saying that, no matter what the circumstances, it wasn't right to defraud family members if we're going to please God.

In the same fashion, my husband gave me a debit card void of my name, with his name only, like a teenager being rewarded for good behavior. How did I feel suffering through such humiliation? Cheated! But God will use everything I went through to help you, my sister, and that's exciting!

In spite of all his shortcomings and the heartache he put me through, God was building my character. As I look back on it all, I can now say I'm thankful and wiser. The peace and awakening formed on the inside of me is priceless ..Happiness, indeed, is an inside job! I had to grow and learn not to take it personally, which was very hard. It took me years to grasp this concept. The fight was not mine to fight; rather I had to hold my peace and allow the Lord to fight for me. There were times I would step back and let Him handle it, and times I took matters into my own hands. That was not an easy lesson for me, because I had a hard time not taking the attacks personally. It was not personal! But then there were times when God was entirely too quiet for me. God didn't send an angel to wound him as he slept, so he could go in the hospital, come out and ask me for forgiveness, then be as sweet as pie, enabling us to live happily ever after. Don't act like you never envisioned this happening to your mate. I'm sure my husband had opinions about me, but God wanted me to allow Him to fight for me. The class was in, but I didn't always get an A+. There was days I got an D+, B-, and there were days I flat-out failed!

He was both infected and deeply affected. I heard someone say that infections are invasions of a thing by an external factor that causes damage. The thing about infections is that not only do they alter reality and degrade the quality of life, they can remain dormant masquerading as something normal and acceptable until they flare up again. Sadly, after I started sharing my experience, I realized that it's a way of life for many women.

Even as I was going through the situation, I was learning. I loved my husband and wanted us to unite and be in sync with God, so we could tell others how God had transformed us and our marriage. So, I stayed in my marriage knowing that one of two things would happen, 1. My husband would surrender to God again and allow God to love on him. 2. God would say enough. At that point, I knew it wasn't time for me to leave. If and when that time came, God would let me know.

God is not pleased when these things happen; He is now rising up to defend covenant marriages. Do you know that the way you treat your spouse is the way you treat God? This behavior is even prevalent among leaders in the house of God. Many of them are preaching and marrying couples but have not yet been delivered and healed themselves, which means they're missing out on God's favor, release, and increase. There is a flow that comes when you have a covenant marriage that's absent when there is no oneness or unity. When you begin to respect covenant, those wonderful things are yours.

When a man has gone through a divorce(s) he has experience in the court system. If he is ordered to pay child support and or alimony, he now has experience in the entire process. Should he choose to rob a woman of being a wife in a covenant marriage because he is still holding on to how his last marriage ended? Example: I'll get married but I won't get a joint bank account. I won't put her name on the house because I can't take any chances; I have to protect what's mine. If he's thinking he will protect himself because he doesn't want to go through he is NOT ready. He is premeditating and living in the past.

Let me holla at the single men and women here: Sir, ma'am, if you enter into marriage with this mindset, you're saying *you do when you don't!* The reality is that you're going into a marriage relationship that already needs CPR, and will soon be on life support, or flat line, if you don't make the necessary changes to save it. You must choose to humble yourself in order to enable that kind of change. Ladies-no one is as capable as God, of teaching you about marriage, so ask Him to give you insight about your husband, or the man who desires to marry you.

When a man chooses to marry and makes vows before God, knowing he has issues that will hinder their unity, he's actually derailing a woman's destiny, and needs to rise up, be healed, in order to live out God's plan for their lives. This applies to women, too.

This pattern can be broken in the name of Jesus. It can be a new day for you and your marriage, but you must renounce your past. In marriage, the first person you must minister to is your spouse. But you cannot be dishonest and minister effectively at the same time, because, you are an enemy to God, forfeiting His favor. God is not pleased with any kind of abuse. Proverbs 18:22 AMP tells us: "He who finds a (true and faithful) wife finds a good thing and obtains favor and approval from the Lord."

Ladies, if your spouse is out of order: staying out late, spending little or no time with you, committing adultery, not praying, or spending the bill money--whatever the issue, fall on your face and cry out to God. Commit to a consistent prayer life--don't wait on your spouse; let it be just you and God. However, I must warn you--this is a double-edged sword, because God is going to work on you as well. While you're praying for your spouse, He is going to talk to you about you, so humble yourself and be open to correction. Don't focus only on your spouse's wrongs. I know, I know this may be difficult depending on where you are in your walk with Christ. It certainly was difficult for me. I thought God was deaf and blind. But trust me, God sees and He knows what's going on in your marriage. What if He is allowing this difficult situation to draw you closer in prayer, to give you the experience you need for your calling or to draw out and birth a nation through you? What if?

Allow God to birth a heart of forgiveness in you so you can see less of what he is doing and hear what God is saying and doing. I know we live in a microwave society, but the change you're praying for may not happen overnight, so choose to be patient with the process. Think about how hard it is for you to change, lose weight, grow hair, gain weight, adjust to being married, stop spending money--perhaps it will allow you to have the grace to partner with God while you and your spouse are growing and changing. I have news for you, no one wants your marriage to survive and succeed more than God does. Will you surrender the fight so He can give you the victory?

Will you prepare your heart and mind to pray this prayer? If you're hurt or angry, take a second and let it go, releasing your spouse to God. Then forgive him so God can forgive you. It may not feel like it, but you're on the same team. The enemy wants to keep you upset and use you to speak against your spouse. It's a setup! Abort mission quickly! It's an assignment from hell!

PRAYER:

God, forgive me for my actions against You and my spouse. Cleanse my heart. Remove anyone who is hindering my marriage from becoming what You desire it to be. God, give me the heart to be humble, to be patient, and to change for the good. Help me to understand what it meant when I said, "I do," which is when the real work began. I surrender to Your process of making me a wife, not just in title, but indeed. Help me to be present in my marriage. I surrender to You so I can be a wife after Your heart. Never allow me to partner with Satan against my spouse. Help me to see my husband as Your masterpiece on the potter's wheel, being formed into a beautiful husband, always protecting the love of my life in word and deed against all others. God, I realize that what I do against my husband I first do against You. Strengthen me. Amen

CLARITY QUESTIONS

1. Do you apologize quickly when someone tells you that you have offended them or do you make excuses for your actions?
2. What do you genuinely need to meaningfully improve about the internal part of you?

Personal reflections

CHAPTER 3

Your lack of healing robs your destiny

Your lack of healing robs your destiny

God wants our lives to be balanced. Our spiritual life should parallel our natural life. People often want power, the gifts of the Spirit in operation, but will not fast and pray for their heart to be healed from past hurts. We forfeit God's divine purpose of going to the cross when we put gauze over our wounds and nurse them. When blood starts oozing, we cover it with fresh gauze. Maybe the wound was a direct effect of being told as a little girl you would never be anything, that you're the black sheep of the family, and it's still effecting you today, years later. What about the physical and mental abuse you suffered as a child and later as an adult? What about the divorce you went through that stifled you? Even now it's hindering you in certain areas of your life, your business, your relationships, and your ministry because of the pain you still carry. What about the anger you experience because your father wasn't present when you were a little girl. God is waiting to heal you. You are valuable. Believers desire to do great things in life and for the kingdom, but it's imperative that we take time to heal, before we can break through to victory in the Spirit. It only takes a short conversation with someone to hear that they are hurt. It's difficult to get wise counsel from a person who refuses God's healing in their own life. Often times they live stuck in the past offenses. Healing is available to everyone! Why forfeit healing but teach about Jesus died for our sins and our healing on the cross? Why forfeit the power in taking communion? It's such a misfortune. You can be a person with power and influence, an entertainer, a doctor, judge, attorney, actress, singer, CEO, a CFO, we all need to be healed. Hurt people, hurt people. But you should be mindful of the fact, because you're in a place of power in the world's system, you must be careful not to allow pride to keep you from humbling yourself in God's kingdom and in your home with our spouse. Get the healing you need and deserve. Pride will keep you out of the will of God—an attribute that's useless in God's economy. He is not a practicing physician. He is the Great Physician.

Some time ago, I sat down with someone who could talk of nothing but how wonderful her services were and how anointed she is. We met for lunch and she snapped a crisp $100 bill out of her wallet for all to hear, don't ask me how she did it, I had never heard a bill make such noise...she had skills..Lol. But all I could see was pride, and it made me sad. When we went outside, she wanted to see if my car was nicer than hers. Really? People, when God allows storms or trials to push us toward healing and deliverance, we need to ask Him to show us the purpose. We often cry and complain about trials, but how many of us would stay stuck in our comfort zones, filled with pride, ignorance, unforgiveness, and the tendency to manipulate others, without them? All those things are strongholds that don't want us to be set free, but when God comes in, we must be willing to let them go, humbling ourselves to become more like Christ. Humble yourself because He truly loves you and wants you to have the healing He has for you. The strongholds entered at some point in your life. The question is, are you ready to be set free of them? Then go to the Father and tell Him you're ready to be set free and let your actions follow. Whatever the issue, it's time for it to go. Old-school believers used to say, "Shine a light on me, God, and if you find anything in me that's not like you, take it out. "Do we still fast and pray to be on point with God? Do we still ask God to cleanse us, so He can use us? Or do we just say, "Here I am, Lord, use me just as I am because I refuse to change." I'm leery of people who always say, "I told God this, I told God that." Isn't it time to stop telling Him what to do and listen to what He is saying for you to do? He wants to tell you something. He wants to give you instructions that will enable you to be free and your prayers to be answered. However, it must be done on God's terms.

Do you recall the story of Naaman, who suffered from leprosy? The King couldn't heal him. Elisha said, "send him to me, and he will learn that there is a true prophet here in Israel." Naaman went to Elisha's house with his horses and chariots, gifts of 750 pounds of silver, 150 pounds of gold, and ten sets of clothes. When Naaman arrived at Elisha's house, he sent a messenger out to him with this message: "Go and wash yourself seven times in the Jordan River. Then your skin will be restored, and you will be healed of leprosy." Naaman, a great hero, was outraged when Elisha treated him like an ordinary person. A proud man, he expected royal treatment. To wash in a great river would be one thing, but the Jordan was small and dirty. To wash in the Jordan, Naaman thought was beneath a man of his position. But Naaman had to humble himself and obey Elisha's instructions in order to be healed. Instead, he stormed off in a rage! He said, "I thought he would surely come out and meet me. I expected him to wave his hand over the leprosy and call on the name of the Lord his God and heal me! Aren't the Abana River and Pharpar River of Demascus better than all the rivers of Israel put together? Why shouldn't I wash in them?" His servant convinced him by asking, "if he had told you to do something difficult, you would have done it. Surely you can do this simple thing." So, Naaman obeyed the instructions, to dip seven times. The Bible says his flesh became as healthy as a young child's and he was healed. Naaman and his entire party went back to find the man of God. When Naaman found him he said, "I know at last that there is no God in all the world except in Israel." 2 Kings 5:5-15

When the very thing you refuse to let go of shows up in someone to whom you're ministering, will you have paid the price for the anointing to set them free? Or to save embarrassment will you ignore the stronghold and leave the person bound? When God wanted to heal you, you ran--you didn't want to confront it. God won't be able to use you to the degree He wants to, because you yourself are still bound. The following scripture comes to mind: 1 Corinthian 13:11 says: "When I was a child, I spoke as a child, I understood as a child, I thought as a child: but when I became a man, I put away childish things."

Children don't know when it's time to mature, which is why we have to instruct, direct, teach, give them understanding, model good choices, and finally, tell them it's time to grow up. There are many people who are mature in age, but immature in the spirit. If that describes you, let me encourage you, let go of the things that hold you back from living out your destiny. You were born to be more than a conqueror.

I have to admit I was very disappointed with my mother-in-law's unwillingness to be truthful with her son. All his life she'd lied to him about who he was. At birth, his mother gave him another man's last name. So, he grew up not knowing who he was as a child, as a teenager, and even as a man. Although he lived in the house with his birth father, he bore another man's last name. He even looked just like his father! When he went into the military, he changed his last name to his birth father's name. But God! When we're unsure of our identity, others will tell us who we are, and not in an affirming way. Many of the issues we face have been with us a long time, but the good news is that they don't have to remain, if we run to God instead of away from Him.

Especially when someone you love and trust deceives you to cover their lies, by giving you an identity that isn't yours, it opens the door for generational curses and the strongholds that accompany them. In our case, my husband sought love in all the wrong places, looking to be validated by his wife while still seeking the approval of his mother. God sent me to stand between the altar and the porch on his behalf, because no one else cared enough to retract the lies and be bold enough to say "I made a mistake, son, and I'm sorry!" Pride and selfishness continued to keep that truth swept under the rug. As his wife, I had to deal with the rage and anger of his past, his inability to trust, his fear of intimacy, and his heart under lock and key. God wanted his cooperation to bring him out. In fact, we were going to counseling when his mother said, "Counseling doesn't work." Neither does exercising if you don't put in the work and close your mouth to the wrong foods.

In reality, he was angry with his mother but took his misdirected anger out on me. At sixty years of age, he's still allowing her to tell him who he is, which is not who God says he is. And she enjoys pushing away anyone else who tries to love him. I am not the first wife she put asunder. In her mind, she is the only woman good enough for him, she was not a mother-in-law who set a good example. She positioned herself as his emotional wife. It was a family clique and as was his custom, he was too afraid to stand up for himself. In reality, he didn't know how, and It showed all over his face in the presence of confrontation with his family. He didn't want to shake the family tree, so he became the victim of family secrets and lies. But our loving Father wanted him to know and stand on the truth that he was designed to be more than a conqueror. Jesus died so that he could be free, a son He deeply loved, even more than I did, because His love is perfect. Early on, someone silenced his voice, trapping his emotions inside, and placing a padlock on his heart so no love could penetrate. The same kind of padlocks were on his feet to keep him moving around in the same unhealthy cycles. He could not share his thoughts, which meant he could not enjoy intimacy with anyone. That endless cycle hindered his ability to commit, as it had through past generations of his family. Something was eating him up inside, but no one could touch it or address it. I lived with what was on the inside. Others saw him as quiet, and assumed that I was controlling him, but in reality, that was false; they could only see in the natural and not in the spirit. I was an abused wife. My marriage forced me to pray and cry out to God.

There are parents who have made mistakes, whose children were deeply affected by their decisions. May I talk to you seriously? Please make it right with your child or children. Please don't continue to sweep what happened under the carpet any longer, walking in denial. Go to them and acknowledge what happened. Set them free. Your apology can start the healing process to reshape their life. Perhaps you were emotionally unavailable because of what happened to you. You may have done the best you could at that time. Or maybe you were repeating negative cycles--habits you were taught; perhaps it's a pattern passed down through generations. It can end with you. Don't die, leaving an internal cancer that's consuming them from the inside out. Be bold, and care enough to set your children free by being honest and telling them the truth, and asking their forgiveness for your part in it.

Sometimes when people have wounds in need of healing and closure, they struggle to move forward and fail to function well. When what they actually need is healing, all you hear is their anger; all you see is that they can't keep a job. They can't keep a marriage, they're addicted to alcohol, isolating you and keeping you at a distance. I recall going over my brother-in-law's house for a small birthday gathering. Before we arrived, as long as my mother-in-law, his mother, was there he refused to come out of his bedroom for his birthday celebration. When she left, he came out, ate and made conversation. He clearly has pain, and he blames her, but she continues the cycle of denial. I pray that he gets what he needs before she closes her eyes for eternity.

#TellTheTruth #SetThemFree

May I speak frankly? Thank you. It's time to break the cycle. And even if no one ever gives you the apology you long for and deserve, please know that you matter; know that you are more than enough. Know that you deserve to be loved, and you are loved by a Father who is greater than any earthly father. This Father gave His only Son to die in your place, so that you could be reconciled and experience true love. Then He said, "I took your sins as my own, when I died on the cross, just for you. I'm going to wipe away every evil deed you have ever done. All you have to do is believe on my Son. Ask Me to forgive you of your sins, follow me, and pray to become like me. Get into a good Bible study, so you can learn to love what I love and hate what I hate. As my Word develops in you, you'll begin to understand Me and how much I love you. Let me say that again: "Love what God loves and hate what God hates." What does God love? What does God hate? There is a lie rising up that wants people to believe sin is not HATED by God. We can't do and say anything we want then say we love God. Don't be deceived. How do you find out what God hates? You read His word, the Bible. Live a life that is pleasing to God. God HATES sin. He loves sinners.

#GodHatesSin #GodLovesSinners

It was good for me that I have been afflicted, that I might learn your statutes. Psalms 119:71

When we face times of affliction, it's time to press into intercession—that is—prayer— talking to God and listening to what He says when He responds. Intervening on behalf of another. Then we take hold of His will and refuse to let go. To do this we must die to our will, desires, thoughts and take on His will according to the Word of God. It's called delayed gratification. Example: if God says to you "Your husband left you, but he is coming home, so accept him back." It doesn't matter what anyone else says or thinks, you take hold of God's will and refuse to let go of what He has spoken to you in spite of what you see or hear in the natural. That's what we mean when we use the term "walking by faith." In order to see and hear in the spirit, we need to be with people who walk by faith. The truth is that we become like those with whom we spend time. But be aware that you'll have to stay in the spirit. When a voice inside of you starts saying that you look crazy, silence that voice and keep moving toward what God spoke to you. Stay on course!

This is why Believers become weary and start to waiver. They have only heard about God's faithfulness; they have only heard His promises, but they haven't stood fast on His words long enough to receive those promises. One after another, people testify about what God will do, but they have no victories to back up what they say they believe. What about you?

Please understand that we will not experience victory or receive the promises of God if we fail to pray and have faith and endurance. Endurance- the ability to do something difficult over an extended period of time or deal with pain or suffering over an extended period of time. The quality of persevering for a long time.

Could it be that we aren't seeing victories and gaining new testimonies because we're copying others who fear to get out of the boat and walk on water at the instructions of the Holy Spirit? Or we talk ourselves out of waiting on God because the opposition is great, and we become weary in well-doing. God will tell you when enough is enough. Until then, keep moving forward until God says, "I am bringing you out. "Have we lost the fear and reverence for God, so we no longer believe that

He knows best? Keep moving forward until God says, "You are out! "Don't listen to the opinions of others. This may take you to a lonely place, but it's a place of certain victory! Raise your shield of faith and trust God.

#YouHaveTheVictory #DoNotStop

CLARITY QUESTIONS

1. How do you react to needed correction when in a personal relationship or within your marriage?

2. Do you communicate when something is bothering you or hold it in, and react unfavorably with a negative attitude?

Personal reflections

CHAPTER 4

Faith + trust in god = winning

Faith + trust in god = winning

Obeying God is a choice, and His instructions will take you to unusual and unfamiliar places. We are living in a time as never before, when we must leave behind the crowds and obey God's instructions to the letter, for our own good. Right now, God is raising up a group of people called the Remnant, who will not buckle or sell out when the attacks come. I'm afraid that there are currently more people following other people than those who are sincerely following Christ. When the people they follow—fall, so will they. It's very disheartening. Will you stand alone in the face of opposition? Or will you just fit in, not to rock the boat while the truth bubbles up inside you?

There is a price to pay if you want to receive uncommon blessings. The bold truth is that you must obey His instructions if you want to see your spouse delivered--if you want to see people healed, families rise up and make Jesus Lord--if you want to experience uncommon blessings and discover who God truly is and His power demonstrated in your life. Abraham obeyed by faith when God commanded him to leave home and go to another land that He promised to give him as an inheritance. In the process of that transition, God moved Abraham away from his pagan family. And not only that, but he went without knowing where he was going. In the same way, it was by faith that Sarah was able to have a child with Abraham, even though they were too old and Sarah was barren. Abraham believed that God would keep His promise, and as a result, an entire nation came from this one man who was too old to have children. In one of my favorite stories, it was by faith that Noah built an ark to save his family from the flood. He obeyed God, who warned him about something that had never happened before. By his faith, he condemned the rest of the world and was made right in God's sight.

The examples of faith listed here, are proof that we can live our best lives through and by faith. The same faith those heroes had then, is still alive and waiting to be accessed today, right now. Where will you allow God to take you by your faith? Whose life will you resurrect? Will you follow His instructions and be the one He uses to lead a nation of unbelievers to eternal life? Will you go from saying, "I do" to become the wife who stands against opposition and prays your marriage through dark seasons, even when you're the only one standing? Will you follow Him by faith to leave a job that pays $45,000 a year, to the place where you own the company and pay others to get the job done? Your destiny by faith is calling you. Can you hear it?

Walk out of doubt and fear. Perhaps you've been told you will never amount to anything. I am here to tell you, that you can and will succeed. Spend time with people who are succeeding. Find yourself a mentor and become what you dream. Ask God to send you one you can trust. Don't become intimidated or jealous of the person he sends. More than likely they will think, live, and operate on a level higher than you. Some women run because they feel inferior, so they end up not excelling as rapidly as God intended. You need them to prepare you for where you are going. A mentor helps you to avoid mistakes that they have made. You can and will succeed! I believe in you.

On April 19, 2017, God said to me in prayer: "My people have put too many limits on Me. Because one person said it is so, people have chosen to believe it. They do not produce the testimony for themselves because they are walking away prematurely. I am God; I turn the heart of man which so ever way I choose. Too many have walked away from miracles based on hearsay and have not proven Me for themselves."

Now that right there, will preach. I hope it will awaken a massive move to take the limits off of God in every area of your life! Too many people say they know God, but those same people deny His power. If you encountered a godly friend who had an answer for everything you went through, wouldn't you hold on to her/him for dear life? Would you not desire them to restore you and stop fear from restricting your life? How about teaching you to have a successful marriage even as you experience storms? Would you implore Him to help you raise your kids? Or perhaps you'd ask her to instruct you how to trust again?

Guess what? You have a Father, and a true friend who can walk you through everything, show you how to live your best life, simply by believing what he says. Please don't remain stuck in unnecessary bondages. Let go of unfulfilled promises from your childhood, your last marriage so you can begin again. Release the fact that you didn't obtain the promotion you deserved. God has already granted you the authority to overcome these things. If you aren't speaking, decreeing and declaring God's promises, you have handed your get-out-of-jail-free card right back to Satan. If you're a believer, what do you believe? Get into your Bible, extract every promise and make it your own. It's past time to stop believing what the enemy suggests and start speaking what the Word says.

James 2: 14-28 ISV tell us: "What good does it do, my brothers, if someone claims to have faith but does not prove it with actions? This kind of faith cannot save him, can it? Suppose a brother or sister do not have any clothes or daily food and one of you tells them, 'Go in peace! Stay warm and eat heartily. If you do not provide for their bodily needs, what good does it do? In the same way, faith by itself, if it does not prove itself with actions, is dead. But someone may say, 'You have faith, and I have actions. Show me your faith without any actions, and I will show you my faith by my actions. You believe that there is one God. That's excellent! Even the demons believe that and tremble with fear. Do you want proof, you foolish person, that faith without actions is worthless? Our ancestor Abraham was justified by his actions when he offered his son Isaac on the altar, wasn't he? We see his faith worked together with what he did, and by his actions his faith was made complete. And so the Scripture was fulfilled that says, 'Abraham believed God, and it was credited to him as righteousness. And so he was called God's friend. You observe that a person is justified through actions and not through faith alone. Likewise, Rahab the prostitute was justified through actions when she welcomed the messengers and sent them away on a different road, wasn't she? For just as the body without the spirit is dead, so faith without actions is also dead."

When you decide to walk away from the opinions of others to march to the beat of the Holy Spirit's instructions, you're ready to excel; in fact, you can't help but win. I experienced people praying with me during my season of trials, but when their faith ran out before my answer came, so did they. I can't stress enough how vital it is for you to step out of the faithless crowd and simply believe God, because those who lack faith will hinder your victory. God's purpose for your life possesses nothing to do with them, therefore don't allow them restrain you. Instead, get excited, expecting God to do for you exactly what He said He would and begin to thank Him before you even see evidence to that effect, because that's what faith is—believing what you cannot see. Stop dragging people with you. By nature, we're accustomed to bouncing things off other people, but there may be times the vision that God spoke to you will be for your ears only in that season. When people start saying goodbye, you cannot take it personally; instead, count it a blessing because in some cases it's God removing your earpiece so you can become His mouthpiece. I'm going to say that again. God is removing your earpiece so you can become His mouthpiece. He wants to teach you by His voice and not their opinions.

DISCLAIMER:

Don't go out and just marry somebody knowing he's not for you, just because you want to be married. You have to be called and graced by God to endure what He took me through. Indeed, God said, to me, "This was the price you paid for the anointing, Write the book." So I did.. smile Though I never told my spouse when God told me to marry him, I wept, but in the end, I obeyed God. It wasn't until June 2016, six years later in prayer, that He revealed the reason why. It was exactly six years to the month He revealed why He wanted me to marry him. It was because God loved him and wanted to bring him out of a dark place. He wanted to use him to help bring his family out as well, but he has a choice in the matter. Ladies pray for your spouse. But remember, your spouse has to be willing and obedient.

Through our union, he was being offered an invitation to return to Christ, but it was up to him to accept it. We started going to church, Bible study, and revivals; we fasted and prayed together as well. He soon appeared to love God and was hungry for the Word. And yet, he still needed to be set free and transformed by the Holy Spirit as we all do. If you're not married and are waiting on your spouse, please don't set yourself up to believe that once someone accepts Christ, all the old habits and sinful thoughts instantly disappear. Deliverance is a process!

At Christmas of 2008, I met his family members. He asked me not to mention the Christmas gifts he'd given me. In fact, I would have to wait until later when we were away from them, to open his gifts. That was an eyebrow raiser, because when someone is mature, they aren't affected one way or the other by the opinions of others. And that makes for a much less stressful relationship. In our case, his family's opinions mattered a great deal more than they should have and severely affected every other relationship in his life.

He was unemployed but was able to still cover his bills by cashing in his savings bonds. Our first Christmas together he actually purchased everything on my wish list, a watch, shoes, perfume from Saks Fifth Ave., and a gift card to one of my favorite stores. I was expecting one of the gifts on my wish list, but not all of them.

Within in a year of being unemployed it all caught up to him. The unemployment office had a check freeze in effect. He was now about to lose his house, car, and credit card companies and bill collectors were calling. I begged him to call his mom to borrow his car note money. He said, "No." When I asked again later on, his answer was still "no." Finally, I said, "You're going to be without a car. How are you going to seek employment and go to interviews? It's easier to come up with the money to repay your mother for two car notes than to have to pay missed car notes, repo fees, and daily storage fees." We who have been there before know, when you're two car payments behind, they're looking for that baby. Finally, he called his mom and she said yes! So, we went on a fast, and God began to send four and five checks at a time during the unemployment check freeze. Then a couple of weeks later another four to five checks rolled in. This happened until he had been paid all they owed him.

It was around Thanksgiving and we were not yet married. One day I was sitting at my computer, and he was looking through a magazine and he mentioned a diamond ring that had caught his eye. He had me pull it up on my computer and we began to discuss the most preferred shapes of diamonds for engagement rings. He liked one shape while I favored another. We talked about the advantages of platinum, gold, and silver rings. He became very curious about one particular ring, so we agreed we would satisfy our curiosity about the different ring shapes and make a point to go view the different cuts in diamonds rings. He argued that the princess cut was preferable to all others.

One day after church we went out to eat. The mall was nearby so we decided to investigate types of diamonds, stones and he once again argued that the princes-cut diamond was the shape of all shapes. We actually went to Kay Jewelers where we looked around, and he mentioned the ring to the clerk who informed us that the ring designer would be in their store in the near future and they would be serving food at a really nice vendor party. We got excited about the food, fun and the games and decided we would return in a few weeks.

The following month we went back for the vendor party. There we learned more about gemstones, enjoyed great food, and met some nice people. While he was off having one of his rings appraised, I visited with the brand Ambassador. As we stood at the jewelry counter, the associate shared how her grandmother had recently passed away. She cried as I began to share the truth about our loving Father with her. In the end, she admitted that she needed to get back to Bible study and fellowshipping with believers. Afterward, we exchanged numbers and even spoke a couple more times in the following weeks.

Finally, Timothy finished his business and when we were ready to leave, he said he was actually trying to finance the ring we admired. To that end, he sat down with the jeweler to discuss the price, financing, and to appraise the ring he brought in. (At the time I didn't know he was going to trade in a ring from his ex-wife toward the balance. In his previous divorce, he lied to the judge and said he did not have the ring. Ultimately, he stated, "they refused to finance him, because the ring was too expensive, and he was currently unemployed." I said, "When the time comes, you'll be able to purchase that ring, or perhaps that will be the second ring you purchase for our ten-year anniversary. But either way God will make a way when the time comes." And I left it at that. Honestly, I thought I would be married at least ten years before I received such a ring. I thought no more about it.

A couple of months later, the day before Valentine's Day in 2010, our church had a guest speaker--a woman of God, a prophetess. She said that when she saw us, she saw one spirit. That same day, after service several ministers agreed, "You two may as well get married today, right now, since everyone is present." When they refused to let the subject go, our pastor agreed, siding with the crowd. I said that wouldn't be happening, because he wanted a wedding. When I turned toward him, he was smiling, but had nothing to say.

That day he was waiting on his unemployment checks, but I had a coupon from Sizzler for a buy-one-get-one-free meal, so we went out to eat for Valentine's Day. Once he dropped me off at my place, he went down to one knee and began to share how much I meant to him then asked me to marry him. To say the least, I was surprised, shocked! I totally thought he was teasing. I said. "But you don't have a ring." He told me to wait, then headed to his jacket. Knowing he was prone to joking, I yelled, "Don't come back with a bread bag tie or a Cracker Jack ring. He came back with the stunning Tacori wedding set we had admired months earlier. I asked, "Where did you get that ring?! Without answering, he dropped back down on one knee and I said, "Yes."

The next month God provided him with a job making as much if not more than he'd been making before. Eventually, learned he was terminated from a manager's position he'd held for years, because his previous wife gave information to his previous employer, saying he had looked into the personal information of another employee. Later I would learn that this was a way of life for him. He was too prideful to ask your permission or for help, so he would do and get what he wanted by sneaking around and accessing what he wanted.

It wasn't long before we started pre-marital counseling sessions and set a wedding date. Our ceremony was nice, but was done on a budget. There are parts I think back on and cringe, because they weren't exactly in line with my love for excellence. But I respected and honored the fact that he wanted a wedding his family could attend since he'd never had a formal public wedding ceremony. We could've used those funds for a very nice honeymoon.

Wedding guests rarely see or hear the issues of the weddings they attend. In our case, three days before the wedding, I got a call from our photographer in Orange County, saying they would be sending a substitute to shoot our wedding photos. When I gave him our deposit, he led me to believe he would be taking our photos. In the end, I had asked to see this the photographer's work, which was not nearly the quality of his work. When I sent over a list of the shots I wanted, the stand-in photographer completely ignored it and failed to shoot those pictures.

When hiring a photographer, if he/she called you at the last minute, to say they can't shoot your wedding, they're actually hiring a subcontracting photographer, giving him a cut of the overall total to work for him on that day. In my case he should have just been honest and admitted that he wasn't available to shoot the wedding.

He didn't want to pass up money, so he hired an associate photographer so he could still make a percentage. At this point, all I can say is that I learned from the experience.

I will also never forget the wedding planner at the church we rented. She tried, but she was very unprofessional, to say the least. I had a long-time client who was going to be my day-of-wedding planner. Everyone showed up for rehearsal the night before the wedding, where the wedding coordinator took over! She refused to allow my wedding planner to have any say. Oh, Lord! I could tell that my friend's patience was wearing thin with her, and it was up to me to keep everyone calm, so we could just get through the rehearsal. I was under the impression that the church's coordinator understood one very important thing: that I wanted the groom to come in during a particular song, while the rest of the processional entered during a different song. That should've been a simple request, but bless her heart, that child had everyone walking down the aisle in the wrong order. I was relieved, however, to see that in spite of all the glitches, everyone appeared to be having a good time at the reception.

After we married, I ended up spending a great deal of time home alone, because he was gone thirteen hours a day four to five days per week for work. He car-pooled, and the commute was over an hour each way.

I will readily admit that there were times we had fun. We went out on occasion, but only if I planned it. I shouldn't have been surprised that as a retired military man, our life was very regimented, which really got on my nerves. As I later learned, he had come by those habits from childhood, where his own father, also a military man—a master sergeant--ran his home with unquestioned authority and expected everyone to obey. His family did what they were told without argument, and that's exactly the way my husband ran our home. It was his way or the highway. Just like his father, my husband did everything on schedule, without a single hitch. He would rise early, never relaxing in bed. Even on his off days he would get up and dressed as if going somewhere, put his keys in his pocket and sit around and watch the television for twelve hours. If he said we were going somewhere at a certain time, and when I wasn't ready at that very moment, he just left me behind. After I went off on him, that only happened once. We never sat down to discuss bills, finances or anything else. When I would bring up those subjects, he would get loud and argue. It never failed. On occasion I would revisit those subjects, but he wouldn't budge. As I saw it, getting loud and pouting were nothing more than a defense mechanism. He was too insecure to be comfortable sharing power, or making decisions together.

Eventually, I began to feel violated in my own home, because he was very secretive and unaccountably sneaky. I repeatedly noticed that he'd record my checking account numbers on a Post-It© note that he hid until I finally disposed of it. Later, when I once again looked in his nightstand, he had replaced it with a new one. Then I dreamed that he had my purse with him in the bathroom and was looking through it. From that time on, I hid my purse before I went to bed. I was puzzled, wondering why he was so enamored with my account numbers, but it would take a couple of years for me to learn the reason.

Not long after that time, we were on his computer searching for vacation destinations. On his computer I noticed that he had saved documents that he used to report someone to the franchise tax board and the IRS. At that time, I didn't think much of it, nor did I have any idea where it would end. One Saturday I came home from a women's fellowship meeting and logged into my checking account online, and discovered that the money from my account and some of the funds from mine and my mother's joint account gone. I went to him, upset at my discovery. I was hot to say the least. I told him what happened and said that I needed him to cover what I needed as well as the money for Mom's medication until they put my money back in the account. He didn't deny anything, he just sat on the chaise looking completely innocent. He never asked questions or denied the incident. God said, "If you fast, I will show you what the enemy is doing." Once I did that, everything made sense--from the dream of my purse in the bathroom, to the documents on his computer. As soon as I could, I called the franchise tax board, and within a few days the money was returned to our bank accounts.

He had no intention of communicating, so that was his attempt to get his way by force. But God had already gone before me, and turned around for good what the enemy meant for my harm.

He was very set in his ways. After we married, I moved 100 miles from my family, friends and the place I called home, to settle in the desert. I tried to get him to move to my apartment in Beverly Hills, but the job he was offered was much closer to the house he was buying.

I often heard his mother say that when it came to men and life, "it was her way or the highway." As odd as it may sound, Timothy was self-centered, and lived out those words in his own life. That phrase sounded good to them, but I can see that, even to this day, it continues to backfire on them. The proof was in the fact that he had divorced several times and run home to Mama each time.

If you're the problem, and you refuse to accept help to change, you will go from one relationship to another, time after time, repeating the same mistakes, and getting the same negative results. I found it remarkable that he simply wouldn't accept that obvious truth. In fact, he would often say to me, "The way I'm doing things can't be wrong, because I've been doing it this way for over fifty years."

My husband was in constant need of accountability, which is why he slowly but surely backslid after the death of our pastor. When it profoundly affected our already-fragile relationship, we went back to counseling with a female Christian counselor who came highly recommended. But after a time, she felt it was important for him to see a male counselor, and he agreed. She suggested we go together for two couple's sessions, so that I could share our issues and then for me to go back for occasional follow-ups with my husband. However, we tried several male counselors without much success. After much prayer, I realized that instead of counseling according to his personality, we needed a man who would give godly counsel according to the Word of God.

We'd been referred to a particular counseling pastor who, unfortunately, would regularly show up an hour late or not show at all. I assumed that he was counseling my husband, but it wasn't long before my husband would come home and mention that he'd spent the time discussing me. When I went with him it was spiritual, and it was helpful. But when it was just the two of them, it was clear that he was definitely sowing discord between us. Knowing that my husband was a babe in the Lord seeking guidance, I felt that the Pastor should have exercised more wisdom.

Over the years I've learned that not all church leaders are qualified to counsel. Counseling should never be based solely on the counselor's experience and clever, persuasive words. Christian Counseling is only effective if it's based on and agrees with God's Word, and that counselor's ability to hear His voice as it pertains to that individual.

Finally, we found a pastor--a bishop, who was located much closer than that previous one, who was an hour and a half away. The new counselor was good. He corrected, gave advice on finances, and offered instructions and wisdom. My husband took the financial advice and used it for himself, but didn't apply it to our marriage at all. The counselor even suggested that if he had to spend $50 to go on a date, it was money well-spent. Tim utterly refused to take the man's advice on dating, to keep our marriage healthy. The truth was that he put very little effort into healing our relationship. When I would make plans for us to go out or to travel, he was a good travel buddy and we would definitely enjoy ourselves. Aside from me making plans, it was work and home. One Summer we made arrangements to go to Maryland to Dr. Mike & Dr. Dee Dee Freeman's Marriage Made Easy, bi-monthly marriage seminar. I arranged for caregivers to stay with mom around the clock, airline tickets were purchased to travel to the East Coast, and our hotel was reserved. He had packed his suitcase. The day we were to leave, he left that morning to go get a haircut and never returned home. Later that afternoon, he sent me an email with pictures attached. The email read, have a good time with pictures of my mom sitting in a chair naked. She had used the restroom and because she was diagnosed with Vascular Dementia, which had progressed so she didn't remember how to wipe herself and she made a mess in the restroom, which said to me he wasn't watching her. I had never experienced her going to the restroom and making a mess. Unfortunately, this was the manner he chose to make me aware of the situation. I felt angered because my mother would NEVER treat anyone like this. I was mad because I couldn't protect her. I was hurt because he was being a bully. My heart was hurt because her dignity was being touched. This was a heartless act.

It had been a while since we were in counseling when I decided to make an appointment for myself with the same pastor, because I wanted to give him an update and I needed to talk to someone who was like minded. I candidly shared that there hadn't been much change. Based on our prior visits he said, "Before you bring him back here, take him to get some professional help with a psychologist, then bring him back to me." He shared his testimony about his previous marriage, saying that, when God released him, he left with nothing but the clothes on his back. I must admit that I thought, *that's not going to happen to me.* Before I left, he added, "Take time to save some money." From our conversation, I realized he was saying that my husband was unstable and unwilling to change, so I might have to make plans to leave.

As the paychecks started coming in from his new job and God was restoring his finances, I discovered that he wasn't willing to allow the check to go into a joint account nor was he willing to give me access to the household account. I had a debit card with his name on it. I found it remarkable when he demanded that I bring him receipts for everything I spent, on the card. But because his request seemed excessive, it was something I wasn't willing to do, and I told him so. He said, "Once I pay off all my debt (in three years) I will then hand over the finances for you to handle." Needless to say, that never happened. At that point, it was clear that he had continued all his old unhealthy patterns, planning for another divorce. I knew deep down that God loved him and wanted better for him. But did he want it for himself?

CLARITY QUESTIONS

1. Did your last relationship result in a painful break-up?
2. If so, are you healed from the hurt ?
3. If no, do you plan to go to counseling?

MARRIED LADIES:

1. Have you encountered hurt and disappointment in your marriage?
2. What steps are you taking to release the offense?

Personal reflections

CHAPTER 5

Marriage needs your energy, focus & finances

Marriage needs your energy, focus & finances

I heard God say, "It's a sin for mothers-in-laws to interfere in what I have joined together." It's clear that God takes marriage vows seriously.

"What God has joined together, let no man separate." We hear this scripture quoted in high wedding seasons, but what does that phrase mean to you?

God created woman for man. After Adam named every living thing, God said that it wasn't good for man to be alone, so He put him to sleep, removed his rib, and used it to create a companion for him in the person of Eve.

When a man marries, he leaves his parents, taking to himself a wife, and their union is blessed by God. The hard truth is that if he doesn't leave, he cannot cleave. Some men physically leave their mothers but are still tied to them emotionally. Have you heard the term 'mama's boy'? It's not as cute as it may sound, because it can become part of a stronghold that is very dysfunctional and can negatively affect everyone and everything in its path. Mothers must understand that they've had years to raise their sons into men, and that doesn't start when they decide to marry. Mothers should depend on what they advised their sons about marriage, trust what they taught their sons about women to beware of, as well as how to treat a woman and what they should expect in return. They should also depend on what they taught them about self-respect. But if mothers haven't prepared their son these things, she has no right to rise as a shield between the son and every woman who enters his life. The marvelous truth is it's never too late to share the path to marriage, but it must be done with wisdom and kindness, and not with malicious intent. Mothers can teach their sons about Proverbs Chapter 5 to give insight. If she has no wise teaching when it comes to marriage there are many resources available. I must declare, it's time for mothers-in-law to cease from interfering with God's institution of Marriage. God said, He is rising up to defend what He has joined together. Remember, God does not join everyone together.

The umbilical cord is cut at birth, but a number of mothers use Gorilla Glue©, trying to put it back together when it's time for their sons to marry. It must be cut in the spirit or the son will be running back to his mother for nourishment when married, when he should be receiving it from his wife's breast. Proverb 5:18-19 NLT reads; "Let your wife be a fountain of blessing for you. Rejoice in the wife of your youth. She is a loving doe, a graceful deer. Let her breast satisfy you always. May you always be captivated by her love."

I remember early in our relationship, my husband's mother was going on vacation to her timeshare RV park in Las Vegas, NV, about a three-hour drive from the house. She was going with her then live-in boyfriend, when she asked my husband to come up and visit her. I thought, *Seriously? ...visit you on vacation?* She lived forty-five minutes away from us, but she wanted him to drive three hours to visit her on vacation. He was unemployed at the time so we drove up and stayed one night. She tried to bribe me to stay longer, offering to buy us dinner. The next morning around 6:30 a.m. she got up to make coffee. When he heard her downstairs, he got up and went to join her there. I didn't know it then, but that's what she expected. I would soon discover that she didn't want another woman being #1 in his life; and she was going to fight to be the only woman in his life.

My husband asked me if I wanted anything to eat, and I said no, because it was too early and I was tired. I eventually got dressed, went downstairs and ate some meat left over from breakfast. Soon afterward, her boyfriend and my husband went to the store, and she used that time to lay down her rules. She said, "When I tell my kids it's time to eat, that is not the time they are to be relieving themselves. It means they are to come to the table." I'm gonna translate what she was saying in my own words: "When I get up at 6:30 a.m. for coffee or breakfast, that means everyone comes to sit before the Princess ." Lol

It's sad but true-- but his mother has hindered him from becoming a mature and responsible man. She then went on to tell me that marriage and God were not for her. So, in her seventies and eighties, she decided to live with a man without benefit of marriage, because she didn't respect the concept of marriage, nor was she concerned for her son's happiness. Clearly, a generational spirit of control was in operation in this scenario.

As wife #3, his mother had little use for me, proven when she told him she wanted gifts that were from him alone, and not from me, for her birthday. She also made it clear that she wanted him to visit her, alone, without his wife. So, he went online and created coupons for her to redeem once a month. For example: Each coupon had a different activity for the two of them. When he showed me his coupons, I was puzzled to see that my name wasn't listed along with his, on the signature line. I was especially confused when I realized that I always had to push him to do something for her birthday or Christmas. I argued the point, asking how he could comply with her demands, reminding him that she would be getting nothing at all from him, if I hadn't urged him to remember her special days. He understood and added my name. When we arrived the next day for her birthday, she opened the package with an expectant look on her face, which changed the instant she saw my name on the card. But that was only the beginning. The tension was tangible when she watched us sit together on the loveseat, and she proceeded to pull a chair up to sit right beside him. Other family members were present, but it was clear they were following the leader and disregarding my presence. That's why even with my own family I don't go along with the clique. And I do not allow negative conversations to alter my opinions. Eventually I said I was ready to go. She smiled as she sat beside him with her arms folded, when he said, "Go ahead and leave," and handed me the keys. In the end, I chose to stay, unwilling to leave as we were dressed to go to our pastor's appreciation service after we left there.

On another occasion, his mother falsely accused me of having a conversation that disturbed her though we hadn't spoken in four months. Unfortunately, my husband was not bold enough to stand up to his family. I find it sad when people allow others to dictate their happiness, tell them what they should or should not do, and even who to marry when it's the right person for their life and God's purpose.

I watched how his family manipulated and took advantage of him. The disrespect they showed him was a little much for me at times.

If anyone tries to separate or divide a marriage, that person is coming against God's designed plan, and will be judged as an enemy of God.

Marriage requires a sacrifice of time, energy, emotions, and even finances. It's important at the outset and during marriage, to discuss your dreams and goals as a family, in order to see if you're on the same page. Write out your career goals, including what they will entail, such as, if schooling is involved, how long it will take to complete, and how much it will cost you to fund it to completion. Why is this so important? Let me give two scenarios with potentially the same outcome, that will have lasting effects.

You have a couple engaged with no clue about each other's deep desires for a career or to further their career. But if they write it out, or discuss it before marriage and draw up a road map, it can save them from future financial stress and eventual resentment. It's easy to become so excited about marriage, that people are willing to set aside their own future plans and dreams, believing that marriage would be preferable to a single life, with a great career. Then within a couple of years or so, they've settled into a routine and suddenly they feel the stirring of that familiar dream. And if they're unhappy in their jobs, it soon becomes intolerable to stay stuck in the same rut, for the foreseeable future. But at that point it may be too great a financial strain to strike out on a new career path, and they have to leave that dream behind, at least for now. As time passes, it's easy to become resentful toward the spouse, who may already have a dream job, who daily shares their excitement about their work, while their mate languishes in broken dreams.

Would it be responsible to take money off their family's table to step out into that long-desired dream, leaving their family unstable, with the repo man coming for the car(s), not enough food to make it from paycheck to paycheck, the phones being turned off, and bill collectors calling, increasing their already self-inflicted stress? At that point, their credit is also in shambles.

On the other hand, there are couples who don't prepare for marriage by even paying down/off old debt, and we were among them. My husband had been employed for five months, after being unemployed for more than two years when we finally said, "I do." At that time, I had a car loan, but no credit card debt, because I had paid them off years earlier. At one point, I had a school loan that I had defaulted on but have since paid off in full. My husband, on the other hand, had so much debt that he took out a second mortgage to pay off debt from his previous divorce, as well as significant credit card debt, a time-share payment and a car note.

After we married, his debt was such a great burden that he suggested we stop buying groceries. I chuckle as I write this, but back then it wasn't the least bit funny when he suggested we eat beans for three years while he paid off his debt, which he figured would take three long years! Was he serious? Absolutely! But I said no way! A counselor had mentioned financial mentor Dave Ramsey, so he began listening to parts of the teaching that he wanted to hear and put into action. Remember, we were newlyweds. In the end, he took money from his retirement account to pay off some debt, so we could buy groceries and live without anxiety. Can you see how it could've caused resentment if he had insisted on having his way? In reality, he did grow resentful at the thought of paying off the balance on my school loan, after he paid off his bills and was still paying the second on his house from a previous divorce.

When people are excited about marrying, sometimes they don't think realistically or count the cost of leaving their dreams behind. Such scenarios can weigh heavily, putting pressure on the relationship. To prevent such issues, it's key to communicate their deepest hopes and dreams early on, with those who will share their future.

Consider this: You don't want what was once a loving, peaceful environment to become a place you dread coming home to. The spouse who loves their career starts withdrawing and spending less time at home because of the stress created by the one who is now struggling.

Don't forget, if you have children, they're learning from your actions and will no doubt follow your example on how to live as an adult. To that end, you must be sure you're modeling godly wisdom and not human folly.

If you're married and experiencing tension and discord in your home, someone may not be broken before the Lord. We can't worship before the Lord and have an intimate relationship with Holy Spirit and He not talk to you about your own issues. You may be singing William McDowell's song "I Give Myself Away," but have you--really? Have you given all of yourself to your spouse? Are there areas you withhold? Are you willing to be open and transparent, so you can serve your spouse the way they need to be served, rather than the way you prefer? Christ gave Himself to us, withholding nothing. Our attitude toward our spouse must reflect the example of Christ, when we say: "I give of myself because I love you." Listen, there may be times you feel that your love is not being reciprocated. Marriage is not based on I do, if you do. But the question is: Can you remain consistent, if you spouse doesn't? That's the God kind of love. Scripture says that when we were deep in sin, He loved us enough to go to the cross, whether or not we want anything to do with Him. That's called sacrificial love. There may be times you aren't making love as often as you wish, or perhaps, for whatever reason, your feelings got hurt. But this is not the time to be selfish and seek solace in the arms, or bed of another; no matter what, it's essential to always choose to love and protect your spouse and marriage relationship. From the beginning of time, it was God's design plan to wait for marriage to have sex. I've said it before, but let me repeat: If your spouse was faithful to God, waiting for sex until after you two marry, he will be faithful to you. I am talking here about a man who fears, reverences, and worships our Lord Jesus Christ.

Don't allow God's best for you be wasted on the illusion of greener pastures somewhere else. Instead, rejoice as you give yourself completely to God and to your spouse.

Did you know marriage is not a 50/50 proposition? The marriage mindset should be 100/100. Some days it may be 80/120, 99/101. But if you trust God, pray, remain patient, and ask God to give him the desire to change, you will see the changes you desire in yourself and your spouse if you **both** submit. Don't forget to be steadfast and unmovable. The definition of the word unmovable: Unmoving, nonjudgmental, motionless. And here's a good one: Unaffected by the feelings and the opinions of others! Set aside your feelings, because they're often deceptive, and can't be trusted. Put all your trust in what Holy Spirit tells you during your prayer time. It's not unusual to trust people, but it's wrong to trust people above God.

To that end, choose to invest time in the process, because disappointment tends to distract us from focus and plant doubt in our minds. Disappointment can cause us to ruminate over what happened until we're focused on the great injustice done to us. And if we stay there too long, we will develop a lack of gratitude and lose the motivation we'll need in our next season.

After I married, I encountered behavior I had never even ever seen before. My mother had always taught us to be kind, and to say please and thank you. Her favorite phrases included: "It's nice to be nice" and "You reap what you sow." I had to decide beforehand to forgive my husband often, to apologize even when I knew I was wronged. I wanted to be forgiven. I soon learned that hurting people, hurt people. I would literally have to make a conscious decision not to allow him to damage my self-esteem or steal my joy. I had to keep in mind that "Happiness is an inside job." When he was mad, I would sing, dance, or do whatever I had to do to keep looking up. In the process my personality was maintaining its dignity, and healing. No one prepared me for this kind of behavior from an adult, but it was the reality I was living. Did I love my husband? Yes, I did. Did I fight for my marriage? Absolutely!

But in my spirit, I could sense a negative force—a deeply-rooted, generational, demonic spirit that fought me every inch of the way. But while I was warring for his soul, God was with me in the battle. It had been there a very long time, was deeply entrenched, and it clearly wouldn't let him go without a fight.

I realized the unveiling had started, when, at one point, he tried to convince me to sell my car and keep his car. But that wasn't going to happen, because my car was paid off. I had also just realized that was a sure way to isolate me, to keep me stuck at home with my elderly mother and no transportation. Who in their right mind would even dare suggest to their wife, a caregiver, to get rid of their car and be stuck at home? Clearly, he had little regard for my well-being. I shouldn't have been surprised, because my husband would rarely apologize, or say thank you. Even the compliments he once gave me, ceased. Most times, depending on his mood, he would struggle after I had made him a delicious meal, and venture a tepid thank you. When our guests would come and lavish compliments on my cooking, he would complement me, because he never wanted others to see him in a bad light. He hid this bad behavior well. Not that we were around a lot of people all the time, but when we were, he was always on his very best behavior. People who came over were my friends or people I befriended in my new city. I refused to allow his bitterness to allow me to become bitter as a result of his harsh, abusive treatment. I had to make a concerted effort to forgive him, sometimes more than once a day. I dared not lose sight of my goal—to please God in all I did, and especially in my marriage. But there was times I filed the test.

Don't allow stressful circumstances to cause you to focus on the negative, or it will hinder your concentration, damage your faith, putting your spirit and your flesh at war with one another. Protect your faith, because, as scripture says, without faith, it's impossible to please God. (Hebrews 11:6).

When the storms of life are raging, you're going to need faith, in order to hear God when He says, "I've got you. I've already won this battle. I've given you the victory on a platter." That's exactly what He told me. His peace envelops you and moves you to another place of trusting what comes from the Spirit of God.

God would let me know along the way what season I was exiting and what season I was entering.

It's impossible to sense all that God is doing for us when we're constantly keeping track of what's going wrong. Stop contemplating the wrongs, and quickly change your focus, or you'll be distracted and drained, robbed of precious energy.

Philippians 2:12 tells us: "to work out your own salvation with fear and trembling."

Growth takes focus, working out to become stronger, bigger. Distractions are sent to change your focus, dilute your efforts and drain you of faith, shattering your hope, and robbing you of your future.

Faith demands focus while disappointment distracts your focus.

Have faith when the storms of life are raging, to know that God is with you and He loves you. I was sitting in church one day when God said to me, "Don't allow your faith to be limited by what I did for someone else, because the truth is that it may have been the limitations of their faith!" So, faith is not a one for all and all for one. Apply your faith, believing the outcome that He promised you. You may have to walk this out, just you and God. There may be times you're believing God, to do just what He said He was going to do, without telling anyone else. Yesterday, I wanted to pick up the phone to tell someone what took place while I was on my fast, but then I heard God say, "Move in silence." You may have to walk this faith walk alone. And believe me when I say that He is enough. As long as you can hear His voice, trust, and believe . . .you can make it through anything. God is still speaking today, loud and clear to those who have ears to hear.

Once when I was talking with a group of people whose marriages had ended in divorce, every last one of them said one of two things: "God told me not to marry him," or "God didn't tell me to marry him." What's the difference in their answers? One, God said not to marry. In the second, the person never sought an answer from God. Never have faith to do something God said not to do. Put a stake in that coffin and walk away, moving forward. Trust God's direction and protection for your life. He knows what you don't know, and can see what you can't see.

You will have a greater level of confidence and security, knowing that God is with you in the fire than waiting until you're in the fire to wonder if He is with you. Know before you go, so your faith can grow.

It's imperative that you hear God's instructions. As you walk through the storm, He'll comfort you and reveal what's going on. I keep a journal with the date and in most cases, I note the time of the most important conversations I will ever have, and that is with my Father. One day God said to me, "I am getting ready to confuse the enemy. He thinks things are going to go one way, but I am coming a different way." Another day I wrote, He said, "I am using this sensitive situation to teach you in spite of what things look like, to take me at my word." He is your peace. No matter what you're going through, allow His peace to fill you, and build your trust in what you learn from the Spirit of God.

It's impossible to sense all that God is doing for us when we're constantly keeping track of what's going wrong. Stop waiting for the other shoe to drop, and look up, so you can remain focused.

In the end, growth takes focus! You'll be surprised how much energy, focus and concentration it takes for women and men to build muscle. You have to drink your protein shake within thirty minutes of lifting weights, to feed the muscle; you have to buy and take supplements throughout the day; you must eat five, six or sometimes seven meals a day, every two and a half or three hours, hit the gym five or six days a week, sometimes three workouts a day, if you're doing cardio twice a day. Then let's not forget meal prepping for most, on Sundays. Focus is key.

As you turn away from what distracted you today, the same thing will not distract you tomorrow. So, go and grow.

I would love to pray with you. God forgive me for keeping a record of my spouse's actions, words and shortcomings. I invite you to teach me to look beyond his faults and see his needs just as you looked beyond mine. Help me to become what you want me to be for my spouse. Perfect your love in me to the point where they see your love living, walking and talking through me. Amen

If you're waiting and believing God for your husband, you can pray this prayer: I invite you to teach me to look beyond my future husband's faults and see his needs just as you looked beyond mine. Help me to become what you desire me to be for my spouse. Give me wisdom, patience, love and understanding for the perfection of our marriage. Perfect your love in me to the point where they see your love living, walking and talking through me. Amen

CLARITY QUESTIONS

1. Why do you desire to be married?
2. The Bible states for a husband and wife to submit to one another.
   a. In your words what does it mean submitting to your husband?
   b. How do you sincerely feel about submitting to your spouse?
   c. Read Ephesians 5:21

Personal reflections

CHAPTER 6

Deception by a husband & mother-in-law

CHAPTER 6

Deception by a husband &
mother-in-law

"Dear Arlisia, the last two years have been the most glorious years of my life, thanks to you and our God. Although, I may not show it now, I'm so thankful to you for saving my life. You've shown me that I have much to live and be thankful for. Your beautiful smile first thing in the morning starts my day off right. The way you worship our God makes me want to love you more and pray that I will have the same relationship with Him that you have. Thank you for being so patient with me and sharing your love for God with me. The second thing that attracted me to you is your classy style. The way you wear your clothes, always getting compliments ☺… to the way you wear your hair (every style is beautiful). I especially love the way you communicate with me and others. The way you speak and your manners shows the world that you are a bright light of God. Thank you for continuing to be patient with me as I learn to communicate better. Thank you for being you and helping me to change into a better person so that we can do the will of God as one! I love you always, Timothy aka Pudty Tat." What a heartfelt love letter from my husband. But it wasn't long before someone got into his ears, and in turn, got to his heart. St. Luke 6:45 NLT reads: A good man brings good things out of the good things stored up in his heart, and an evil man brings evil things out of the evil stored up in his heart. For the mouth speaks what the heart is full of.

Soon it became obvious that my husband was having an affair(s), committing adultery. I found out he liked porn and meeting young ladies in their early twenties. I once saw him on a website for cheating married women, which could be why he started locking his cell phone and keeping it on him when he was at home. Once I told him I hired a private investigator because he would get up early on his off days and leave without explanation. He abruptly stopped for a good while, after I made that announcement. Maybe it was because he felt guilty, but for whatever reason, he began sleeping on the couch. Why? He said his back hurt when he slept in the bed. I suggested we purchased a new mattress to make him comfortable. He didn't want to spend the money.

One day he went out of town for work, and I called his hotel room, but got no answer. I repeatedly called his cellphone, and again got no answer. I was concerned so I called the front desk and asked if they could check on him. When they did, he answered the door and told them to tell me he would call me tomorrow. I could have gotten on a plane, instead I wisely decided against it.

When my husband went to work the afternoon of December 8, 2016, the events of December 9th would forever change our marriage.

During the week leading up to that day, he was unusually peaceful in the mornings, and he even chatted while we had coffee, without me having to ask questions to get him to talk.

There were two occasions that I know of, when he had a work holiday and was off those days that he didn't tell me about, so I thought nothing when he left for work at his usual time and returned thirteen hours later, at two a.m. God allowed me to find out that he was absolutely off work that day. When I asked why he hadn't mentioned his day off, he answered that he didn't know he had to. I was so mad that I broke his glasses and threw them in the trash.

December 9, 2016, I woke up close to three a.m. and noticed the light in my mother's room was still on, which meant my husband hadn't come home from work. I always left the light on for him in Mom's room, and he would turn off the lamp and turn on the night light when he went in the closet in her room to change for his shower. It wasn't often he would work overtime, but when he did, he didn't like to call home to inform me, though I repeatedly asked him to.

When I went downstairs, there was no sign of him anywhere. I called his cell phone and his ring tone for callers was Adele's song, "Hello", and the lyrics played "I must have called a thousand times to tell you I'm sorry for ever breaking your heart." I thought *okay, who is he playing this song for?* This was new and not the norm; apparently, he was now paying for ring tones for someone and the lyrics were not for his wife. After calling him a few times I could tell that he shut it off, because it started going straight to voice mail. When I called a few minutes later, it was ringing again, so clearly, he was trying to ignore me.

Then I called my husband's job and was told he left with his rideshare partner who was a co-worker. His co-worker said he would call and check on them, but it wasn't long before he called to say that Tim didn't answer his phone. However, he did reach his rideshare partner and was told he dropped him off at two a.m. Knowing Tim as I did, I knew he wouldn't be excited to learn that his work knew his business. In fact, being retired military meant everything to him, so much if they told him not to cheat on his wife he would comply.

The next morning, it was just after six a.m. when we heard the noise at the front door. I said 'we' because not only did I hear it, but my cat leaped up, startled, then ran downstairs with me following close behind. I had placed a chair against the door so I would clearly hear when he arrived. I could only assume that since he couldn't sneak in, he jumped back in the car and left. When I looked out the front window, I saw our car at the corner, getting ready to turn right, he turned left instead. He didn't call me; he just left me hanging.

As time passed, I grew more upset, wondering where he was, and when I finally called his mother, four hours after he usually gets home from work, she said she hadn't heard from him and would call me if she heard anything. That evening, I called again, and my call went to her answering machine, so I proceeded to leave a message, saying I was going to file a missing person report. Hearing that, she picked up then put me on hold to brush her teeth. When she returned, she sounded concerned and said she would get back to me if she heard from him. She knew I hosted my women's fellowship the following morning, and she even offered to watch my mother during that time, which was not like her at all. I declined her offer with my thanks, but the whole situation seemed strange. She said, call me in the morning. I called again the next morning, and again I got her machine. By then, I was pretty sure she knew something, but had no intention of telling me.

I couldn't imagine what would make a husband think it was okay to just run away, moving on to the next relationship without saying a word, and feel justified. As I would soon find out, that's exactly what he thought.

Ladies, healthy relationships require open and honest communication, so develop your ability to communicate. When we don't speak, clearing the air, we open doors for the enemy to enter and do his best to destroy relationships. The enemy knows he has us trapped when we hear and perpetuate a lie that sabotages relationships, if we don't shut it down. In my experience, very few people like to confront or be confronted in order to protect friendships or the marriage relationship. If you do make the effort to confront, some people will respond negatively, deflecting, and dismissing the issue entirely.

And if that happens, it becomes a vicious cycle where nothing gets resolved.

Even in church, people will hear gossip and negative words, and because they refuse to confront things according to God's Word, the body of Christ begins to self-destruct, preying on each other instead of offering love and support. Matthew 5:23-24 states: "So if you are standing before the altar in the Temple, offering a sacrifice to God, and you suddenly remember that someone has something against you, leave your sacrifice there beside the altar. Go and be reconciled to that person. Then come and offer your sacrifice to God."

Communication is also essential in the workplace. Initially, we use communication during the interview process. And when we're ready to leave, good manners dictate the need to communicate with a conversation or a letter to that effect.

Communication is just as important in ministry. When a person enters a ministry excited to be there and say, "The Lord advised me to come here for you, to hold up your arms and intercede." We must be faithful to honor the instructions, whether it merely means showing up in prayer, and undertaking whatever God has instructed us on their behalf. A span of time past, people start talking negatively in your ear or you hear about another ministry opportunity where you can shine and you disappear.

But the Lord told you! As much as we might not want to detect it, the truth is, if you keep leaving ministries without the respect of a conversation with the pastor, you become recognized for being unreliable and a person with communication, character and a integrity issues. And if that's the case, we should pray, asking God to change us from the inside out, so that we're open and honest before the Lord and everyone else. We must remember that our name and reputation will go places we will never go. Our good name should precede us, making way for us because it's so excellent.

The Friday my husband didn't come home, he didn't have to return to work until 2:30 p.m. on Monday. And though he had three days off, he didn't spend them at home. I ended up hearing from a young man my husband had previously worked with, who said word had gotten around that Tim hadn't made it home. He was obviously concerned and rightfully so, so he sent a text to check on him. The following morning, Saturday, he called to say he'd received a text from Tim, saying he was okay.

Three days later he was back at work so I decided to call, and he answered. When I asked how he was doing, he replied in a nasty, bitter tone, "I'm fine!" I knew he had someone behind him, reinforcing his bad behavior, so he could justify it. When I asked where he was staying, he said, "I have a place to stay." I responded, "Why are you talking to me as if I wronged you?" At that point he could do one of two things—either humble himself and own his actions or turn the tables and play the part of victim. Since he never owned up to anything, it was useless to continue the conversation, so I hung up, feeling frustrated to say the least.

The following week I remembered that I'd made my husband a doctor's appointment for the following Friday, which was coming up soon. The appointment was near our house. It would be one week since he left home for work, after which he had cut off communication entirely.

When that day arrived, I went to the appointment but made sure he didn't see me. There they were together—he and his mother. All along she'd been saying she had no idea where he was, but right then she was sitting beside him, telling him she was excited about his birthday (four days hence) when she would take him out for a steak dinner.

I should've figured it out—he'd ended up back at her house, as had been his custom over the years. A short time later, I parked at her house and was ready to greet him when he parked his car in her garage. It was the first time we'd spoken in eight days. When she exited the house, to see what he was doing, I said, "Shame on you, Mother Staley. You said you hadn't seen or heard from him and you'd let me know if you did." Caught in her lie, again! She quickly turned and ran back into the house. Clearly, she was enabling his bad behavior and had no intention of changing.

At that time, his mother was eighty-two years old and had no respect for our marriage relationship. In fact, she had always done whatever she could to divide us. She told me years earlier that marriage was not for her, and that she was better off living with a man, because marriage would only mess things up. If that's what you believe, don't continue to force your disrespect for marriage on your son and his wife. Needless to say, Tim's mom didn't respect her son's marriage and didn't want to see him happy and fulfilled unless it was with her. At almost sixty years old, he still wasn't ready to mature to stand up to her and do the right thing.

We were still standing in the garage when he said, "Come on" as he got into the car. I was thinking we were going home, so I turned to pick up his work boots. When I turned back toward the car, he sped off. I headed into his mother's house, because it was raining outside. When I opened her back door, the security alarm went off.

The next thing I knew, my husband texted me to say the police were on the way, because he had called them. His mother appeared just then and said, "You know, sometimes my neighbors call the police when they hear my alarm go off." Shaking my head, I said, "He already texted me to say he called the police." She had once again lied, trying to cover his revolting behavior.

I called someone I know, who lives nearby, who was also a deputy sheriff, to come and pick me up.

It wasn't long before police arrived and asked for my husband, and his mother said he wasn't there. She got into this story and told the officers that it was none of my business what they do. She went on to say that she never meddles in her children's business. By then, it was clear that the police were getting tired of waiting for my husband to arrive.

When they asked her what was going on, she told them, but as usual, it wasn't the real truth. One officer asked if I lived there. I said that I didn't live there, but was waiting on someone to pick me up. Then he asked her if she would mind if I waited inside, and she shook her head, but said he could bring a chair outside for me to sit on. It was dark, cold and still raining, so it wasn't easy to find a place to stay dry. As the police were getting ready to drive off, my husband came walking up, and I knew she had notified him. I asked him if we could talk, but he snarled, "No!" Then he disappeared inside his mother's house, and left me waiting outside in the cold for my ride home. I never attempted to contact him again.

I didn't have too long to wait outside and found a place to stay dry.

At that point, I had to choose to keep a good attitude, knowing that happiness is truly an inside job.

It's in the time of testing that you see what's really inside you, not in the absence of a storm.

In Romans 8:38-39, the Apostle Paul said: "For I am persuaded, that neither death, nor life, nor angels, nor principalities, nor powers, nor things present, nor things to come, Nor height, nor depth, nor any other creature, shall be able to separate us from the love of God, which is in Christ Jesus our Lord."

We often quote this passage, but the Apostle Paul lived it out. There is an enormous difference between quoting a cliché' and sharing a testimony. Paul had been through the test, letting no one and nothing separate him from the love of Christ.

At that point, I too was walking through the same kind of season—letting nothing separate me from the love of God.

Whether it feels like it or not, God is not our enemy when trouble comes, so we dare not listen when the devil tries to convince us that God has abandoned us. The Book of James (Life Application Study Bible) Chapter One reads: "Dear brothers and sisters, whenever trouble comes your way, let it be an opportunity for joy. For when your faith is tested, your endurance has a chance to grow. So let it grow, for when your endurance is fully developed, you will be strong in character and ready for anything."

My faith was being tested and it was time to allow my endurance to grow by submitting to God and refusing to let bitterness develop inside me. When in the gym, I was good at building endurance. But, what about in my personal life? My heart was involved. I loved being a wife, cooking and preparing meals from scratch, and making sure he had lunch to take to work. I even waited up in the early morning hours to hear how his day had gone at work. I loved entertaining, cooking and decorating the house for the holidays. I also enjoyed it when we had opportunities to travel together (he was my favorite travel partner). I truly believed our marriage was going to be changed. I had to totally lean on the Holy Spirit to comfort me when things went south in our relationship. And He did just that!

Learning to trust God's process is a process. When my husband decided he was going to do what was best for him and revert to his past dysfunctional behavior as a single man, it was a test. It was clear that no one but God could change someone; it had to be his decision to except or reject the opportunity.

Have you any idea what it takes to be patient and remain sweet and teachable when you're being betrayed, with no end in sight? It demands that you allow your flesh to die when you get to this point. And though that sounds daunting, once you choose to do it, you'll be filled with the peace of God, knowing that He has your back. Most of us are use to handling things in our own way, with our own strength. In fact, at times it seemed that God wasn't moving fast enough to suit me, when I would be tempted to take the situation into my own hands, to make things happen. But when I chose to wait on God and trust in His timing, I had more peace and those old thought patterns just fell away like a snake shedding its skin. Unlike humans and other animals, snakeskin isn't flexible, so a snake must leave behind the old skin, in order to replace it with a looser skin that offers room to grow. In the same way, we must shed our old mindsets to make room for us to grow in grace, and become more like Christ. Thank God that He helped me with my choice to wait on Him.

I received a prophetic word from a Woman of God on New Year's Eve, a few weeks after my husband left; in it, God said, "I am vindicating you. I am preparing you for ministry. I am qualifying and covering you. Get your journal out and write. More love will come out of this that will help other women who struggle. What the enemy planned for evil, I am turning around for your good. Your husband has fallen deeper into sin. I was protecting you by keeping him from having sex with you. Your meal barrel will never run dry. God has you so tough. At that moment, I thought, yes, he does. It's amazing how much peace God has given me through this. Rejoice. God said to praise Him, because it's a new season! God is going to uncover what's done in the dark and it's coming to light. God said, "You love covenant."

CLARITY QUESTIONS

1. If you saw the person who hurt you face to face, how would you react?
2. Do you become defensive when a true characteristic is pointed out about you?

Personal reflections

CHAPTER 7

Dear mama

CHAPTER 7

Dear mama

For years my mother had always been affectionately known as 'Jew." Sitting here I've been thinking about her, and several things come to mind. I never heard her curse, pass gas, which was the ultimate no-no in her book, drink alcohol, smoke, or turn down orange soda and a good meal. She wasn't just kind to her family, but to complete strangers as well.

My mother was very nurturing. If I took sick, she went above and beyond to make sure I was comfortable, saying, "Baby, you want some soup?" She would come into the room every so often asking, "How do you feel, baby?" Once after I was grown and had moved out, I went to the emergency room accompanied by my sister. After I was released, I returned to my mom's house, and she gave me a bell to ring if I needed anything. When it cracked me up, my sister said, "That big ole bull don't need a bell." Meaning, I was not a baby. After that I rang it just to get on her nerves. Mom would come in to ask, "What you want, baby?" All three of us would crack up laughing.

Mom had a strong belief and would often tell us, "You don't live with a man if you aren't married. Why would you buy the cow if the milk is free?"

My parents were well-known in the neighborhood as those who helped raise an entire generation of neighbor's children and grandchildren. Looking back, though I can remember seeing her upset, I never saw her enraged or out of control. She had certain rules I've never understood, including, getting us up by eighty-thirty or nine on Saturday mornings, to get work done around the house. She didn't mind if we took a nap after the work was done, but she didn't want us to laze around in bed all day. She was also recognized for traditionally cooking delicious dinner almost every day, though on many Fridays, we typically got to eat at McDonalds or Dad would bring home fresh fish he eagerly bought from a co-worker who went fishing. My parents would then work together to clean, scale, gut, and prepare the fish. And to this day, I can still remember how great it taste. My brother and I made homemade French fries to accompany the fish, which were equally delicious.

One thing was for sure in our home, when we were growing up: We went to church. If you wanted to stay home because you weren't feeling well, Mama wouldn't let you go out to play later. So needless to say, we didn't stay home from church much at all. There were even times when, if you didn't eat your vegetables, you couldn't go out to play that day either.

Dad was a deacon and Mom was a deaconess in the church. In Dad's later years in life, he was ordained a minister. Even when his doctor revoked his driver's license, he still found a way to get to church services.

Our neighborhood was a fun place to live, and provided many wonderful memories. That was back in the day when kids played outside until we smelled like little puppies needing baths. My dad was known for keeping the greenest lawn on the block by fertilizing and continually watering the grass, often while I was outside playing. I will never forget the day my dad stood by the garage and called me, and I ran to see what he wanted. He had caught a grasshopper in his hand and when I got to him, he removed his thumb off the grasshoppers' head and showed me, knowing I was terrified of those things. Needless to say, I ran away screaming. In spite of tricks like that, I had the greatest parents in the world.

This story takes my mind to later years when I was grown up and was vacationing in St Thomas. We were riding in the back seat in the resort's van with the windows down, of course, and the ocean breeze blowing. The next thing I knew a grasshopper flew in the window; chile, I'd never moved so fast in all my life to get away from it, which made the van driver laugh. In his distinctive Caribbean accent, he said, "Grasshoppers are good luck." Yeah. But since I don't live by luck, you can keep your grasshopper! LOL!

After my marriage my mother, would come to our home to visit so I could spend time with her. I feel that it's nice to make time for your parents especially as they get older. These days, young folks don't have time to slow down for the aging. Technology has us speeding and doing everything at an accelerated pace. Technology is changing at a rapid pace that older people can hardly keep up. I enjoyed having Mom with us for the holidays. She'd been big on holidays for as long as I could remember, and I wanted that tradition to live on through me. I needed her to know that I appreciated all the years she invested in making our home a stable, loving place. She made the holidays memorable for me with all the holiday cheer she could muster. Oh, how I miss her those times of the year. Thanksgiving is a week from today, and if she and my late sister were still alive, we would be discussing the dinner menu for that special day.

When mom was still cooking, our house was filled with the aroma of delicious food, including two to three meat dishes, and seven to eight desserts. For instance, coconut cake, jelly cake, sweet potato pie, gourmet gelatin mold, sock-it-to-me cake, butter pound cake, and 7-up cake, all from scratch. That's a whole lot of sweetness. Then there was the traditional dressing, mac and cheese, yams, green beans with white potatoes, greens, corn bread, gravy, and the list goes on. But there was nothing traditional about the taste. It was all cooked with love. In fact, the food was so good that family members who were Jehovah Witnesses would come the day after Christmas to indulge.

During the summer of 2013, I hosted a women's retreat. Then God said, "After the retreat, take a week and rest, then go get your mom and nurture her. I picked her up the end of June 2013, and never took her back home, knowing she would have three square meals a day living with me.

Contrary to what my siblings believe, I didn't plan to keep her indefinitely, when I took her to my home for a two-week visit. But I wasn't going to return her home unless God said to do so. My love for her and my commitment to God just wouldn't allow me to do that. It saddened me to realize that my siblings didn't feel the same way. But by then, I had her with me, and I was going to obey God and nurture her.

I found the following entry in my prayer journal after Mom passed. "God said, 'Protect your mother.' " When I saw it, I was stunned, realizing that my spirit had accepted the assignment though my flesh had forgotten all about it.

I was taking care of my soon to-be ninety-three-year-old mom with help from my husband. I appreciated him for that and would thank him and would often give him tokens of my appreciation. On a couple of occasions, his mother tried to stop him from assisting with Mom's care, saying she needed him to come and help her with her step-father since she had kicked out her live-in boyfriend. But we knew that it would be impossible because her step-father could no longer walk at all. It was time he went into a facility, but she tried to use that ploy just the same.

My mother was easy to be around. She and my ex-husband would play and go back and forth. He would irritate her (he was known for being irritating, even with his co-workers) I would have to tell him to stop because they sounded like two kids teasing each other. He would tell her she needed a job--that she needed to get up and go to work. She would reply in a no-nonsense tone, "I don't know what you talkin' about, I worked for years —don't need no job." When I would run errands, sometimes I would sneak out of the house and she would ask him, "Where is that girl?" He would call me on the phone and put her on. I would laugh and ask him why did you call me? Knowing she was going to ask, Why didn't you take me with you, when are you coming home? By the time I returned, she would be fine. Sometimes I just needed a little break.

During that time, I introduced Mom to the song: "Let the Church Say Amen" by Marvin Winans, and that became her favorite song. Mom could be in the middle of something and I would turn on her song and she would smile from ear to ear. If she was seated, she would have her legs crossed singing and moving her head side to side.

Before I moved her in with us, there were several times when my husband and I discussed bringing her to live with us and he was all for it. But we never sat down and put a concrete plan together. Honestly, I didn't plan or see it happening. Neither of us truly knew over time what that would entail. Three years into my marriage God told me to bring my then eighty-nine-year-old mother to our home and nurture her. What I thought was going to be for two to three weeks turned into four years and three months. She'd been diagnosed with vascular dementia many years earlier, but when she first arrived, she was able to function pretty well with a little help. She was kind, giving and loving, and even in her time of need, she was polite and respectful. Then, as the years passed, I watched her health decline. I must say it was one of the most difficult things I'd ever done. One day God said to me, "I trust you-- that's why I chose you to care for her." Even in that, it was difficult because of a troubled spouse.

If we allow Him to, God will prepare us for what is to come--even for the passing of a loved one. One day after putting Mom down for her nap, I was lying on my bed resting, and I heard God say, "I'm going to take her." I screamed, "No!" We all want our loved ones to be healed, but we must ask and listen to what God is saying about the situation. When we become one with what God is saying and willingly move in that direction, the peace of God fills us and carries us through. Truly, this is the result when we allow Him to be God, and trust that He knows best. When we're believing God to heal our loved one, we must ask if that sickness is unto death. We all have a time to depart from this life. If His will is to take them He wants to prepare us for that season as well. But ultimately, we must back up and allow Him to be God. Did you know that God won't go against the will of the person for whom we're praying? Find out what God is saying about the situation at hand, or if the ill one is praying to go home. If His desire is to take them home while you're still praying for healing, you're missing out instead of letting God prepare and strengthen you for their transition. He'll give us strength in every area of our lives if we submit to Him.

One thing was for certain--I was going to do as God had instructed, caring for my mom until her spirit life left her body. When my husband left, God kicked in and gave me the strength needed, day-by-day to do what was necessary for my mother. Five months after he left, her health began to decline in earnest. Daily I would give her a shower, brush her teeth, lotion her, dress her, administer five breathing treatments per day, meds in the morning, meds at night, and walk her daily if it wasn't too hot or cold outside. Eventually, she was no longer eating three meals a day. Dementia progressed and robbed her of the ability to remember to swallow, so she would chew and chew endlessly, so that one meal took an hour and a half if not two. Over time she could handle eating only once a day.

After seeing the same doctor for thirty years, she was ready to retire, which was fine, because it took ninety minutes to get to her office. And in an emergency, it would've been much too far to drive.

The doctor I preferred was no longer taking patients, so I settled for the person in that office who was still accepting new patients.

I wanted to make an appointment so he could see her, discuss her meds, tests, etc. But when we arrived, he never even greeted my mom, which was far from the norm for Kaiser Doctors. In fact, he didn't say a word to her or touch her. Before we left, he told me that in the future I could just call instead of bringing her into the office. As you can imagine, as soon as I could, I changed doctors. Looking back he could have been looking out for my wellbeing as a caregiver.

The sad truth is that we can't leave the responsibility for our health in the hands of our doctors. We must ask questions and more questions to make sure we leave with an understanding of our ailments, treatments, meds and their possible side effects. For example, you should ask: What a particular medication is for, and what side effects, you should watch for. And you should know that you don't have to be discharged from a hospital if you feel you or your loved one is not ready. You may insist on them staying an additional day or two if their diagnosis and condition warrants it. They will escalate your concern to the proper department by law.

One day I noticed a sore on mom's foot that would not heal, though she was not a diabetic. I took her to a Kaiser clinic near my home that had an Urgent Care clinic that was open until nine p.m. The podiatrist gave her antibiotic pills to take three time a day with meals.

NOTE:

Caregivers often have so much to remember that they may not think of appropriate questions on the spot. When I told the doctor that Mom wasn't eating three times a day, it was apparent to me that she couldn't take pills with food three times a day, and couldn't take them on an empty stomach. Within a couple of weeks, her toe was worse.

The podiatrist there only worked part time until noon a couple of days a week. At that time Kaiser was in the process of adding an additional podiatrist, and boy was it needed, to get in within a reasonable amount of time. I called about Mom's ongoing wound, but instead of calling back, I was referred to the nearest specialist fifty miles away. The day finally arrived to see the specialist only to learn that the first podiatrist had neglected to recommend steps required prior to the new appointment. In essence, she should've been seen by another doctor and had X-rays taken. So that day we had them take the X-rays before we went home and had to schedule an appointment to see the doctor she was supposed to see initially. He also ordered a liquid antibiotic, which is what the first doctor could've done instead of giving her pills.

When the day came for her next appointment, I got her dressed, but by the time we were ready to leave, she could no longer walk, and would never walk again. There was nothing else I could do but cancel the appointment. But now I had a new and more pressing problem--her bedroom was upstairs.

I couldn't help but wonder how things would've turned out if the original podiatrist had done things right from the beginning. To accommodate her changing needs, I had only recently ordered a hospital bed, because her previous bed was huge, and made it difficult for both of us. The new bed was also much safer for her—a big improvement.

The first priority of caretakers must be the personal comfort of the patient, even to rearranging furniture for their comfort and safety. We are accustomed to our loved ones being the shot caller. As our parents age, we need to step up and make life decisions for them. Such as, making sure they use a walker, buying socks to prevent their feet from being cold, purchasing appropriate and comfortable shoes for them. It's critical to realize when they can no longer be at home alone and swiftly improve their environment. One fall can lead to their death.

Neither of my parents ever wanted extraordinary measures to prolong their lives. Years earlier, during a short hospital stay, the practicing doctor asked Mom what she wanted to do if her condition demanded extraordinary measures. She responded she didn't want to be on life support. She said, "if I leave, do not bring me back." My siblings and I almost fainted in unison, she agreed to artificial life support, but only for seven days, to be turned off after that time, without fail.

When her condition worsened, I had to make the decision to put Mom on palliative care, then on hospice. It was clear that I wasn't the best caregiver on hospice, but I did the best I could. Kaiser's Hospice told me not to call 911 when something happened; they wanted me to call them. One morning, I called hospice at four a.m., but got no answer, so I left a message. By noon, I hadn't heard back, so I called again, then waited forty-five minutes for someone to answer when I called.

In the end, I decided to call paramedics to take her to the nearest Kaiser Hospital with an emergency room which was about fifty minutes away. I packed my overnight bag with a few days of clothing and followed paramedics to the hospital. I have to admit that I stopped at McDonald's, knowing that they would have to get her processed and find her a bed before I could see her. I would always stay overnight with her, whether it took three days or ten. And since she was no longer eating or getting enough nourishment from the Ensure she drank, I wondered about the need for a feeding tube.

It's important to know why your loved one is reacting differently when there is a change in their condition. As it turned out, my mom was not herself because of an infection. Once the Emergency Dept. admitted her, I spoke to the doctor on duty about a feeding tube. He didn't think she was a good candidate based on how she was looking and reacting. I shared with him that it was due to the infection. I disagreed with him, so I called a couple of people I knew who had experience with loved ones on feeding tubes. Both of them had positive experiences. Once I prayed, I decided to go for the feeding tube. People make feeding tubes seem like the worst device in the world, including one pharmacist who had no knowledge or experience with one.

After Mom was given antibiotics and fluid to hydrate her, she was a different person—she was her old self again. The same doctor was all excited the next day, saying that she knew her name when he asked. That's why it's so important to know your loved one for yourself. I had to make the best decisions for Mom's care. Once they're gone, we either live with peace or regret. When her time came, I knew I would have zero regret and a whole lot of peace, knowing I had done my best for her. It was worth it all to have that time with my sweet, beautiful mother.

With what time she had left, I made sure she knew how much I loved and appreciated all she had done for me. While she was living with us, I started videotaping her, recording her voice when she sang, and taking photos, creating memories that would last a lifetime.

At the Kaiser Hospital we used, ER doctors worked seven days straight before they were replaced by other physicians. The next doctor was God-sent. When his grandma was living, she too was on a feeding tube and all the grandkids were trained to operate it. He told me what type of dresses to buy to accommodate the apparatus. He had the nurses show me how to use the machine while she was in the hospital. He was one of the best doctors I'd ever encountered, so I made sure to leave a positive feedback with the hospital administration. I was in Mom's room with the admins present when I told them if I ever opened a hospital, I would look for him to come work for me. They laughed, and he appreciated the compliment. We often look for supervisors to register our complaints, but I always try to take that same kind of initiative to give a compliment.

I took her home and the next morning I felt overwhelmed by all the new information I'd seen and heard, so I left a message requesting him to call me, and he returned my call only moments later. To reassure me, he said, "Don't worry. You're going being a pro." He went on to explain that families are usually too intimidated to take their loved one home on a feeding tube, so they put them in care facilities, where the patients are put on medications to sedate them if they feel they are too busy or troublesome. I will forever remember and appreciate his comforting reassurance.

From that point on, I cared for Mom from her hospital bed. My entire routine had to change, because I'd never done it before. I changed diapers, turned her every few hours to prevent bed sores, and because I didn't want her to feel like a burden, I would often say, "I love taking care of you! I'm going to care for you for the rest of my life. I want you to live forever!" Frown lines would form on her forehead, which was her way of saying, "Nobody lives forever."

Eventually the lack of circulation in her foot caused dry gangrene, which is a form of coagulative necrosis that develops in ischemic tissue, where the blood supply is inadequate to keep tissue viable. It is a not a disease in itself, but a symptom of other chronic conditions.

Daily I would have to properly apply Betadine, allow it to sufficiently dry, then wrap it with sterile gauze. Ultimately, it spread from one toe to all five toes, then up the shaft of her feet. The Betadine would dry it out, and the toes would get hard, which helped. They warned me that her toe(s) could possibly break off if they became brittle enough. And though I was always apprehensive when I carefully unwrapped it, I was incredibly relieved when it didn't happen. During that time the hospice nurse would come to our home a couple of times per week. Some days I would wait for her to arrive before I unwrapped the foot, grateful that someone was there with me, I did not want to unwrap the gauze and be frightened and because it really required more than two hands to hold on to and rewrap it.

Imagine walking through this situation alone in the natural. God was definitely there for me! God kept me, He held me, He sustained me, He comforted and strengthened me! He is our hope, our joy, our peace, and our stability. It's far too much pressure to look to a single human being to be all those things, because, according to the design plan of God, we need Him to be our hope, our joy and our peace. People can give us a limited amount of help and support here on earth, but ultimately, they can fail us, so the backbone to all our peace and stability, absolutely must be from God. We mustn't hold people to a standard or a place that only God can fill. We can trust them--we can love them, but ultimately if they fail us, we must have already put God in first place in our lives and make Him our priority, to come through victorious. Man is frail and has clear limitations, while God is our Sustainer. If man does fail us, we can fall back in God's arms. It may hurt for a season, but remember that God is a healer, and He remains a deliverer. When He's in His proper place in our lives, the disappointment is not as great as when we place people above Him. It was never supposed to be that way. God is our all and all, He is everything we need Him to be. We must make Him Lord, so that He governs over every area in our lives.

It wasn't long before Mom was no longer taking anything by mouth, so everything was put through the feeding tube, which worked remarkably well for her.

Eventually, she stopped talking, but she understood me, and if I asked her to smile, she would.

On another occasion, I took her to Kaiser Hospital because one side of her face was swollen. The only way to get her out of the house was to have paramedics come upstairs and put her in a body bag to carry her downstairs to a gurney. One time, even though I had thoroughly explained how they would have to carry her downstairs, they sent two small girls, and I had to help them carry her, we had to lay her down at the top of the stairs, but we made it. I would always request for her to be transported to another Kaiser Hospital since the closer Kaiser had no emergency room in the building. And thankfully they always agreed.

When we arrived at the hospital ER, they didn't want to treat her. I requested antibiotics and fluids to hydrate her, because when they can no longer eat or drink orally, they easily become dehydrated. Two doctors in the ER told me that I needed to take her home to die. I asked when was she going to die, how much time she had, and they said she might have a couple of weeks, and one admitted that he wasn't God. That was my point exactly. When I asked for a second opinion, he said, "I am your second opinion." I stated I would like a third opinion and that I would return. On the back of the admitting paperwork there is a number to call to dispute a prognosis or a discharge if you disagree.

I went to my car to pray and decided I would not fight, but would go ahead and take mom home. As I began praying God stopped me, and said, "Take solace. I know what's best for your mom." When I returned, the floor nurse was there and he said, "I understand you would like your Mom to receive antibiotics and fluids?" I said, "Yes sir." He said, "That should be no problem." When I politely asked if he would admit her, he said yes, that he would send in the doctor for her unit. Soon the doctor for that shift came in, carefully examined her, then said, "What's the big deal? The worst thing that could happen is the antibiotics don't work." She sided with me in the end she was admitted.

Once mom was admitted and moved to the hospital, the next morning the unit doctor was sent in to speak with me regarding not bringing my mother back in since she was on hospice, and I kindly but firmly thanked her, and said, "I only have one mother." I knew the time would come when it would be her last trip to the hospital. The few times Mom was admitted, I became acquainted with the staff and nurses. As we were ready to leave after that visit, I thanked them and said it would be our last visit. They would often say that Mom was lucky to have me, but the truth is that we were blessed to have each other.

On Wednesday, August 30th, the day before Mom's birthday, her pastor drove out to see her with a couple of the church members I'd known all my life. I had her smile for them. I couldn't help but be grateful that they'd taken the time to visit.

The following Saturday I cleaned her up and, as it turned out, she never opened her eyes again. Her breathing started to change as I had read it would. I called hospice and they sent out a nurse by the name of Steven. He had an excellent bedside manner and was very informative. I asked him if it was time and he said, yes. That night after he had left, I was nervous about the process. Her breathing became increasingly labored. At 12:16 a.m. I called 911, moments later a sheriff deputy arrived at my home. His official name is SGT. Monroe, I know God dispatched him. During our meaningful conversation I realized he too was a believer. He was patient, kind, and understanding, as he walked me through my options, which I found comforting. He stood right there by my side as the medics checked my mom. It was becoming absolutely detectable the personal dilemma I had to face, these were moms last hours or day on this side of life. Metaphorically speaking, it was more tolerable having someone hold on to my hand. He remained at my house for more than an hour. I had a DNR (do not resuscitate) order in place for Mom, because that's what she earnestly desired. I was not going to be selfish and try to keep her alive in a compromising state. She was unafraid to die and made it known over the years. With no code in place, EMTs could do nothing in the event she went into cardiac arrest. I called for them to come just the same, I was a bit nervous. An angel remained by my side, he recognized the sensitivity of my loved one leaving this side of life, for that I am thankful and grateful. Later a second deputy showed up, out of concern SGT. Monroe assured me if desired one of them would remain with me. I told him I was fine, and they both left. I genuinely did desire him to stay, but I felt I was imposing.

#GodSentAnAngel

Sunday was more of the same as far as her breathing was concerned. I started to feel she would not last through Monday. That evening I called my siblings to let them know that Mom might not make it through the night. One of my sisters said that she didn't want to see her like that. My brother said he would call me the following day. My other sister said she might come the next day. I went to rest at two a.m., and at three-thirty, I got up, and glanced over to see that her chest was no longer rising with each breath. When I touched her, her legs were still warm to the touch, and I wondered if she had just passed. I called hospice, who sent out a nurse to pronounce the time of death. Soon the mortuary came for her body. After bagging her they covered her with a green velvet blanket and wheeled her out for the last time. She passed four days after her birthday. Once again, God's Holy strength kicked in and comforted me like you would not believe--a faithful and true friend and Father.

I learned a great deal watching my mother as I cared for her. No matter how she felt, she was always kind and thankful. As I write this, tears of gratitude stream down my face, knowing that God chose and trusted me to be the one who walked her to the door, while He stood on the other side to welcome her home.

If you have ever been a caretaker for anyone with love and compassion, you know it's a serious undertaking. I love when I hear of a family coming together, taking shifts to keep their loved one at home. But, more often I hear of bickering, while one person out of an entire family tackles the task alone. Why does this happen?

The excuses are many and include: I can't stand to see them that way; I have a job that prevents it; I'm married while my sister/brother is single and has nothing better to do with their time. I live too far away. Please hear me when I say that few people understand the physical and mental stress of constant caregiving, without breaks or respite help. If you really love your parents or love one, you will offer to give the caregiver a weekend off by stepping in to help. In fact, studies have shown that the stress of caregiving often ends up severely affecting the caregiver's health, and even causes premature death, and they sometime pass before the person they are caring for. And please don't salve your conscience by stopping in once in a while to say hello. That is no help, at all. In my experience, the failure to step up and help is based on laziness, unforgiveness issues for past offenses, whether real or imagined, toward either the patient or the caregiver.

If you have a family member who is tenderly caring for your parent or loved one, willingly give them breaks on a regular basis. It can be two weekends out of the month, or siblings can trade off and cover different weekends, even if it intentionally means missing church to make it happen. This is your parent, too. Love is what love does. God's Word says the greatest gift is love. I sincerely believe God would rather you willingly miss a service and show love toward your mother, father, sister or grandmother in their precious time of need. If not, please consider splitting the financial responsibility with family members to pay for a respite worker to come in and assist with the tireless responsibility. This will provide rest for the caregiver, that would be an enormous help, and mean much better care for the patient. Fondly remember, you yourself may need this kind of care as you age, so have compassion enough to help your own loved ones while you can.

CLARITY QUESTIONS

Find two scriptures in the Bible regarding forgiveness and record them here. If you don't know any Google scriptures on forgiveness.

PART 2:

Write down the name(s) of people you need to forgive.

Choose to let go, release them of the wrong they did to you, so you can move forward. This is for you, not them. Sometimes people move on and we hold them hostage in our mind and heart.

Personal reflections

CHAPTER 8

Enough! Is! Enough!

CHAPTER 8

Enough! Is! Enough!

As I go back through my prayer journal, it's clear that God was strategically working on my behalf, so I want to share those entries with you. Keep in mind that I was still married and living with my husband at the time.

March 22, 2015: I parked to go in and pick up my mother's prescription. Since it wasn't ready, I sat in the backseat of the car, where God began to speak to me and said; "I have spoken to your husband again and again to change. And because he will not, I am going to deal with him one-on-one because I am obligated to you." Several times He repeated the phrase, "I asked him again and again to change." He was speaking like a father who was left with no other choice.

December 13, 2015: In prayer God said that a whirlwind was about to come and shift my life.

December 17, 2015: God said, "In twenty-one days, a shift is coming."

December 23, 2015, I was in the midst of my two-day preparation for Christmas dinner. I turned my head to look around the kitchen and the family room. It was as though I was in a fog. I felt a move. I opened my mouth and quietly starting saying good-by good-bye. I heard God say, "You're moving on to bigger and better things." I remembered thinking: Are we moving to a new house, are we going to purchase our first house together?

January 10, 2016: God said, "I am moving for you, fighting for you. That's why the enemy is fighting you in prayer. You shall win!"

January 12, 2016: (Happy Birthday to me!) On my birthday God said, "I am going to walk you through this, so you can minister to marriages and help them."

May 31, 2016: God said, "Fast for three days. After the fast there is going to be an explosion."

June 1st thru June 3rd I fasted.

June 2, 2016: I was lying on my bedroom floor praying when I heard The Holy Spirit say, "A move is coming." I wrote in my journal the following: (is that a new home?) I was hoping it was with my husband.

June 8, 2016, God said, "I am giving you the VICTORY, so you need not fight. I am turning it around. I am giving you strength, so use it wisely, use it wisely. What I am doing for you, you cannot imagine. Eye has not seen."

June 15, 2016: God said, "He is losing momentum. I put you two together to bring him out of a dark place. He has rejected me and my servants I have sent. Prepare yourself, prepare yourself."

July 22, 2016: I went to a hotel for a two-day shut-in with God.

July 23, 2016: I heard God say, and this is what I wrote, " I am releasing you, for you have served well."

(marriage?) What? (I couldn't believe what I was hearing.) "He made his choice. It wasn't you or me, it was him. It's time to move on. The best is yet to come. I will walk you out of this." When I heard that word, I left for home shortly afterward. But I was still in disbelief, so I put it in the back of my mind. But in the future, I will believe what I hear even if it sounds unreal.

July 31, 2016: In prayer I heard the Lord say, "Take refuge in me. He that dwelleth in the secret place shall abide under the shadow of the Almighty." Refuge - condition of being safe.

I had a vision of court documents. When I woke up, I told my husband and he was quiet. I knew from what God was telling me that he had been planning the divorce for some time now.

August 4, 2016: I had just finished my coffee and raisin bagel when God spoke, "The battle is not between you and your husband, it's between him & Me (God). Everyone will know that I am with you. This is your season now!! You will laugh and be happy. You will not be sad! You have made mistakes in the marriage, but I have forgiven you. But you have served well. You have gone from battle to battle to battle; it was part of your training. People will know that I am with you."

October 2, 2016: God spoke to me: "Think it not strange that I have brought you to this place (marriage) because I brought you here. I am removing the stress. I am bringing you out! Many will call you to minister because of what you went through. Let go of the stress that is created by you trying to pull while he is pulling away."

The following journal entries was after my husband had departed from the home.

July 1, 2017: As I woke up this morning, I heard God say, "I am not taking you out, I am snatching you out."

September 11. 2017, 9:00 p.m. God said, "This is a very strategic time, this is strategy time." But because I was upset and frustrated, I asked God, "If you say I am out of the trial, why are all of these darts and arrows still coming at me?" God answered me: "I am carrying you. Imagine if I wasn't--you would be dead." Then I wrote; Thank you and across half the page I wrote; "I WOULD HAVE FAINTED UNLESS I BELIEVED TO SEE THE GLORY OF THE LORD IN THE LAND OF THE LIVING!"

Then God said, "Take heart, daughter, for I am walking you through this. I have given you the VICTORY. But the VICTORY is not just going to come; you must follow the instructions to the place of the VICTORY, because VICTORY has a place." Did you hear that? VICTORY HAS A PLACE—so don't stop!

* A lady was sharing with me she embraced a friend who is praying and believing God for her marriage, just as I had been. I suggested she share my book with her. She said, "but your marriage ended in divorce. I said to her, "many people are under the misconception if what they believe God for does not manifest the way they desire then they've tragically lost the battle. Extraordinary victory has a place. As long as you are hearing God, and

carefully following His specific instructions to the end of the trial, where ever you end up is your place of victory."

This is why some people stop believing God, they don't believe effectively. You must believe what God is saying to you and not hold on to your own desires. God will give you insight to your situation, that is what we must believe and pray. Do you recall this scripture? "I tell you with a certainty; whatever you prohibit on earth will have been prohibited in heaven, and whatever you permit on earth will have been permitted in heaven. Matthew 18:18 ISV

When you follow God's leading, you can undoubtedly look for your ultimate reward and restoration here on earth! I am a living witness.

If you do not keep a prayer and dream journal, please start. There is so much God wants to communicate to you. I record every prophetic word I receive. Trust me, I play them back at the right time and I am so encouraged. Some of the prophecies I had forgotten. There is no way we will remember the important words from Holy Spirit as the days and years go by when we're facing discouragement, days when our faith is wavering, or when we are facing the enemy or in a battle. The mind was never designed with 65 GB of memory. It was never designed to store data. That's what recording devices, pen and paper are for. A recording artist records his songs, but as time passes I have heard them say, "I forgot the lyrics to the song." Without singing it for an extended period of time, the artist can forget the lyrics. But they can always refer back to the original recording. Free your mind and start to journal.

When God said He was giving me the victory, a great deal was happening in my life, but as I read my journal entries, I realized that God had done exactly what He promised. Now I could see that He'd been protecting me all along, and was now removing Tim from my life because he chose not to respond to God. And just as God said, He was obligated to me, to my happiness and my future, because I had followed His lead. All I could say at that moment was, "Wow! Thank you, Father! You never cease to amaze me."

December 2015, we were at a birthday/Christmas celebration, and a woman of God said to me, "God said keep a journal. "I was journaling and continued to do so. If I had not obeyed God and reviewed my journal entries, in order to recount my story, I would've believed my husband left me, and suffered feelings of rejection. (There were times when rejection tried to speak to me. I quickly shut those voices down.) But that's not what happened. God removed him. With that current information I could align my thoughts and emotions with what God essentially did.

And guess what? In the same way, He is obligated to you and your happiness and all that pertains to you as long as you get into and remain in His will. Psalms 84:11 NLT says: "For the Lord God is our sun and our shield. He gives us grace and glory. The Lord will withhold no good thing from those who do what is right." Being in His will means it will *not* be as you please, at **your** discretion, as you see fit, at **your** pleasure, at **your** desire, at **your** whim, at **your** inclination, or according to **your** wishes.

His will is **as He sees fit**. This is what it means to trust God: in order to be a believer, a Christian, you surrender, giving up *your* will because He knows best. He is God, the Creator. Whether they realize it or not, most believers follow their own will and wonder why they aren't getting the results God promised in His Word. If this describes you, examine your heart to see whether you're living out your own will, or have died to your own will in order to submit to God's will. You hear a lot of people thanking God, but only the redeemed can truly worship Him.

What about divorce?

It's never God's best plan. No one wins in a divorce. Everyone loses something.

Marriage is not a game! Ladies, the harsh truth is that love is not enough to guarantee a happily-ever-after scenario. If you marry a man who hasn't been trained to value integrity in the areas of manhood, relationships and marriage, it can be a more difficult journey than necessary. If all he has seen or experienced are broken promises, womanizing, and an absent father, etc., beware, because the red flags abound here. Under no circumstances should you rush into marriage, especially when you see red flags. Allow God to direct you. For your own good, you should desire a man who is led by God, committed to God, and passionately worships Him—a man who is broken before the Lord. I said it before, but it bears repeating here: if he won't cheat on God, he won't cheat on you. If he is truly submitted to God, he will be committed to you.

Remember, "Happiness Is an Inside Job." Ladies, if you want a happy, enduring marriage, it's time to seek God in fasting and prayer for your own personal healing, deliverance and flourishing spiritual growth. You want to be able to discern the correct husband God has for you and not allow the devil to steal your destiny by giving you a counterfeit of the real thing. It's time to put in the work. Many women are desperate to be married. Some women have said they would rather settle than be alone. If they do that, I hope they make it out in their right mind, because divorce can destroy you physically, mentally and emotionally. Divorce is death! Guard your heart. So, if your heart is broken allow yourself to heal, or you will take brokenness and hurt into your new relationship. You will be drawn to a man who appeals to your brokenness. Your judgement will be off, leading you to make unwise decisions. The stories are endless, of women who were miserable because they settled for less than God's best.

If it were up to me, pre-martial counseling would be required by law, before marriage. In my humble opinion, if a couple desires to divorce, they should be required to attend counseling for a minimum of six months—okay—once a week for three months. Perhaps the institution of marriage would be taken more seriously. What do you think? Do you feel that the divorce rate would decrease under those circumstances?

When we divorced, I would be my husband's third ex-wife. He used the same attorney for the first two, but that Attorney had since retired, so he had no choice but to hire a new attorney to dissolve our marriage.

I have to admit that I was perplexed to realize that women desire good, loving men to marry, yet those same women raise their sons to be anything but good men. They raise them to be exactly the opposite of the kind of man they themselves would want to marry. They spoil them, they side with them when they do wrong; they refuse to act according to truth, or give them tough love. Ultimately, they enable their sons' bad behavior; then when the sons marry, those mothers stay involved in their sons' business, disrespecting the marriage boundaries. Shame on the son who's not mature or bold enough, to keep his extended family out of his marriage. Bro, you have to man up. Ladies, before you marry, before you get serious with this guy, be sure he has healthy boundaries with his family, and especially with his mother. A good mother-in-law will understand she is no longer first in his life. Within the marriage relationship, his wife is now priority number one. And his family shouldn't give him grief for his decision to marry.

NOTE:

Don't let desperation motivate your actions. Sis, at this point it's important to slow your roll if a man shows interest in you. Watch and listen to find out if he is God's will for you, or if you're merely settling. Don't be afraid or too desperate to walk away if it's not God's best, even if you've already started to plan a wedding. A canceled wedding is better than a scheduled divorce and all the pain, devastation, expense and inconvenience that goes with it.

God spoke to me clearly when He said, "I'm getting ready to deal with wicked mothers-in-law." Let me be quick to add: That does not exclude Christian, church-going mothers-in-law. Mark 10:9 NIV tells us: "Therefore, what God has joined together, let no one separate." And He means just that. Many people have come between what God has joined, and God requires that a price be paid for such disobedience. If this describes you, it's time to sincerely ask God to forgive you and help you change your behavior. Are you willing to change your heart and ask Him to forgive you?

God made me so tough!

During the most challenging time in my entire life, my husband left for work and never returned home; he also refused to speak to me once he left. Four months later, he filed for divorce, the same time I was caring for my rapidly-declining mother who required full-time care. I also had to pack up and look for another place to live, because he was buying the house before we met. My mother passed, leaving me to plan her homegoing only one month before I had to be out of the house. Even after making a concerted effort, I had yet to find another place to live. But God! He literally held me together, showing me what it felt like to have a truly loving Father to carry me through the storm. He strengthened me so much that I didn't even cancel our monthly women's ministry meeting during that trying time. And although I didn't mention what I was going through at the time, it was clear that God had my back!

It was clear that the attack was designed to take my mind, kill me. Yet after all I'd been through, because of His faithfulness, I've grown to love and trust God all the more. God was literally holding me. He covered me, encouraged me and walked me through a terribly challenging season in my life. Put another way, I experienced God's strength as I never had before, and He wants to do the same thing for you. Many people have mental breakdowns or worse, after going through what I experienced. Did it feel good, No! But it is pushing me toward my purpose. Do I understand God's ways? No! But I do trust Him. I love Him more each day. Isaiah 55:7-9 NLT tells us: "Let the wicked change their ways and banish the very thought of doing wrong. Let them turn to the Lord that he may have mercy on them. Yes, turn to our God, for he will forgive generously. My thoughts are nothing like your thoughts, says the Lord. And my ways are far beyond anything you could imagine. For just as the heavens are higher than the earth, so my ways are higher than your ways and my thoughts higher than your thoughts."

I hate divorce, because, unfortunately, divorce occurs as the result of a hardness of heart. If divorce must take place, couples can really save thousands of dollars if they simply communicate and come to an agreement about cars, finances, children, property, etc. Imagine the money you could put in your pockets if you set aside pride, to agree on the important things.

I know of several divorcing people whom family law attorneys have cheated out of money. Even my attorney is trying, but that won't happen! When I hired him, he was advertising in the city where I live, I later discovered that he advertises in every major city in the Southern California. He is a former district attorney for San Bernardino County, and he has satellite offices in different cities.

I have to admit that I was more frustrated with the way his office is run than I was with the whole divorce process—well, not quite, but I was convinced that my husband had a more professional attorney, and that's a really bad feeling to have about your own attorney. I jokingly say, my husband had a part time job hiring lawyers.

I will start by saying that my attorney, was initially gentle and soft-spoken, and seemed knowledgeable, thereby gaining my confidence. One other thing—his bio said he worked in his church. After interviewing several others, I decided to go with him.

Doing my due diligence, I made an appointment to interview him as well. I returned to his office another day to say I would like to go with one of his associate attorneys, because I could not afford Mr. P at $500/hr. rate and the associate only charged $300 per hr. But he promised that the $500 fee would apply only when he went to court.

Very early on I became frustrated with how he ran his office. His office manager and paralegal, was very unprofessional. For instance, I was told that I didn't need to show up for court, because one of their attorneys would go to represent me. Five days later, with less than twenty-two hours' notice, I was told I needed to show up in court the next day. They had known for five days, but decided to call me at the very last minute, knowing that I was a full-time caregiver for my mother. They knew it wouldn't be easy for me to find a sitter, and ultimately put me in a very bad situation.

I showed up in court the following day and waited for an attorney his office hired from near where I lived, who was an hour and a half late! No one had even attempted to call me.

No one kept me informed on my case or even replied to my emails, so I always had to call the office for updates. I had to wonder if he knew how his office was being run. In the end, I never mentioned it to him, because it would cost me $500 an hour for the privilege.

I had to call to find out if the office manager was communicating with my ex's attorney, looking for dates we could meet, but that begged the question, "Why would you contact them with meeting dates without first consulting me, your client?"

I was receiving phone calls for paper work that I already given them on several occasions. I often stated, "Do not charge me for this call." My divorce was final two months before I was even informed that it was so! The frustrating thing was that the same attorney never contacted me twice; it was like a revolving door—never the same person calling. Even now, I'm convinced that he hired them as temporary workers or hired case by case, which is okay if your office can keep track of who's doing what so the client is not billed twice for the same work.

I raised concerns about money my soon-to-be-ex was hiding, but my attorneys never pursued the subject.

When I inquired of my attorney about this issue, he said, "Well, you wanted to keep costs down." True, however, I should have been given the options and costs, to explore my concerns! You give your client options, costs and let them decide the best way to spend their money.

Our settlement meeting was held at my husband Attorney office, which was the first time I had seen or spoken to him since December 2016. My attorney was running late so I sat out front until he arrived. There was a room set aside for use by my attorney and me, and once he arrived, he escorted me to that room, and I looked up to see my husband, who stood up and said, "Oh, you look nice." I'm sure my appearance didn't reveal the struggle I was having, packing up to move, cleaning the house and garage, and trying to find a new place to live.

Let me digress a moment right here. Ladies, no matter what you're going through, look your very best, and refuse to wear your pain or disappointment on your face. Buy a new outfit, or at least a new blouse, and fix your hair. Be sure to do your makeup. Then get a pedicure, or do something else special, so you'll feel better about yourself. You do not have to look like what you've been through!

When I went to shake my husband's hand, he hugged me. He asked about the animals and made small talk. We were very cordial. Our attorneys were going back and forth, negotiating our divorce, so they left the room and returned on several occasions. And while I could've been very anxious and upset during that time, God was faithful to give me an abundance of confidence and peace. I made sure to lie before the Lord in the days leading up to that day, so I wouldn't sit in the meeting a sheer mess. Woohoo! It worked!

Our case was open and shut. We didn't argue, oppose, or go to court. Even my attorney said my case was very easy. We decided on an office hearing. My attorney had explained the cost to finish my case and wrote it down, then we both took photos of the paper. He went in to ask my husband's attorney to pay my fees. His attorney said *no way*. From what my attorney said, our local court didn't allow their clients to pay attorneys' fees of the other party. I thought that was pretty hard to believe, and I knew my husband could afford it.

In the end, my husband had two months to submit documents, while I had to be out of the house sixty days after that date. My husband said to him, "I can have it in two weeks." My attorney should have argued that I still needed sixty days from the agreed date, but because my counsel just went along with what was said, I had to be out a month sooner than I'd planned. And in the midst of this situation, my mother passed, which meant that I had to plan her funeral, bury her, find a place to live and move, all within a very short span of time.

I was expecting a check from my husband's attorney that would go to my Attorney's office. When the check arrived, I asked his office the deposit amount, but no one would tell me. They just kept asking for my bank information in order to send a wire for the net amount they planned to send, once they had deducted their fees without once speaking to me to answer my questions. Finally, the office manager said she would make an appointment for me to talk to my attorney. When I spoke with him, he said it would cost another $4,000 to finish my case. He stated a little extra was withheld in case some unforeseen reason additional work was required. I argued that he had already quoted me a much lower amount then increased it by $1800. When I responded, "What? More money, more money, more money," he took offense.

At the end of our conversation he said his rate was *increasing* by $50 per hour for any future work, but he didn't say that the increase would apply to the very last stages of my divorce. Because I demanded it, he put into writing what it was going to cost to complete my case and said that if there was any money left, he would issue a refund. (Like that would ever happen.) When I asked if he had ever issued a refund before, I could tell he was outraged that I'd even asked the question. He reluctantly said, Yes, he had.

In the end, he billed me again for the amount he deducted from my check. The money he subtracted was supposed to complete my case. As of today, I read new reviews from his clients, who also claim he vastly overcharged them. It's time for people to take action against fraudulent business practices by taking their complaints to their local Bar Association and the Better

Business Bureau. After my experience, I found that this misconduct is far too common and needs to stop.

CLARITY QUESTIONS

1. Do you have a lot of debt?
2. If yes, what measures will you take to pay it off, if possible before you get married?
3. If you have not paid your debt off before marriage, will you inform your future husband before you get engaged, after you become engaged or after you are married?
4. Please explain your answer to question #3.

Personal reflections

CHAPTER 9

My new beginning

CHAPTER 9

My new beginning

"*I would have despaired* had I not believed that I would see the goodness of the Lord In the land of the living" (Psalms 23:13 AMP).

Part of the divorce agreement dictated that I had to move out of the house because it was his house prior to our marriage. At that point, it became clear why he never wanted to put my name on the house documents. There is one thing I know about God--He has always given me better than what I previously had. I started packing to move in September of 2017.

I did not know where I was going, but I had to be out of his house no later than November 1st. I was searching online looking for a place that I found safe, comfortable, and located in a nice area. Every place I found required renters to make three times the rent, debt-to-income ratio had to be low, etc. My soon to be ex-husband was only giving me $500 monthly. I said God, I need to meet the owner of the house or the realtor.

In January 2016, God told me to start saving money and I did! I didn't know why, but I was well aware that it would affect either my destiny or that of someone else. I realized that if I disobeyed His instructions, I could not hold Him responsible for my outcome. Whatever you do, learn to love and obey God's instructions whether or not they make sense or are comfortable or easy. They will be a lifeline, the answer to your prayer.

I went and looked at a few houses, and even a few apartments, which would have been a step backward for me. Not that I have anything against apartments, but from experience I was determined to stand for what I desired and not except less.

October 2, 2017, was a rough day filled with frustration and tears, after I went to look at a house that wasn't for me. I wouldn't settle for it, as urgent as my situation was. I was in my walk-in closet where I went to pray, when I got off the phone after having a Christian sister agree with me for the right house. At that point, I heard the Lord say, "I sent an angel to your new house." I leaned back in the closet to relax and He said, "I heard everything you've asked for. I am answering, I am manifesting the house."

I kept looking at houses. I was on the phone with a young lady from the ministry, and she went online and pulled up houses, then mentioned one I had decided not to see, because the pictures didn't appeal to me. I called the next day, asking to see the house and the call went to voicemail. I called back that evening and a gentleman said there was a lockbox on the door and I could go visit at my convenience. So, I immediately went to view the house. I walked inside, went from room to room, and instantly fell in love with the place. All of a sudden there was a knock on the door. I asked who it was, and he answered that he was the owner. I opened the door, and he introduced himself as the realtor. We quickly hit it off and ended up talking about ourselves and our lives for a half-hour, then he offered me a lease application and I took it.

I invited my sister in the Lord, Leighla, to see the house. When we arrived, it wasn't long before we lay on the floor talking and laughing, because she too, really loved the house. We went and sat in the master bedroom closet till we broke out in prayer. She stated, "God said it was going to be a haven for Him to dwell." In fact, I was so excited about the place that I drove by often in the following days and even went back at night to check out the quiet neighborhood.

Each time I went by the house, the dispenser for applications was empty or almost empty. Within a couple of days, I filled out the application. I went to my prayer closet to pray and God said, "Get up! Go turn in the application. "I have already worked it out." This is what the scripture means when it says that faith without action is dead, (James 2:17 NIV). God was saying to get up and put some action to my faith! As believers we must put some performance to our faith, because God is often waiting on us, while we are waiting on Him. Nothing will happen if it's our move and we fail to follow through. We dare not allow fear to hinder us, saying we're waiting on God. If that happens, we will miss our season(s).

On October 6th I faxed the application. On October 7th I emailed it. On October 8th I received a call from the Realtor, who said he was meeting the owners and he would tell them that he wanted me to have the place. (Keep in mind that I felt he was actually the owner). Then he asked me to fax over documentation. Well, I had income that was ending and income that was about to begin, which I chose to explain. This is where the obedience paid off.

On October 11th, I received a call from the owner of the house, who said, "If you're still interested in the place, I would like to offer it to you. I chose you because 1. You made a good impression when I met you. 2. You were ready to move in. 3. You had good credit." On Friday the thirteenth I had the keys in my hand, which was great, because I had plenty of time to move before my November 1st deadline. I cleaned the house to my liking, moved in my new appliances. And, the house was as large and had more upgrades than the house I left behind. If I had believed Friday the thirteenth was bad luck I would have missed out on my blessing.

Let me recap: on October 2nd, God said He'd sent an angel to my new house. On October 6th, I turned in my application. On 13th, I had the keys in my hand. The miracle manifested in ten days. This house was exactly what I asked God for, a single-story house, with four bedrooms, three baths, a two-car garage, and it even included the services of a gardener. It was the same square footage as my previous home. All this because I followed the instructions of the Holy Spirit.

When I moved in, He provided me with the appliances I desired and so much more. It has been a haven. I love coming home--so much so that I miss its peace when I have to be away. I love it! And I love and thank You, Father, for You are faithful.

#WhataFaithfulGodWeServe #YourBestDaysAreAhead

When God brings you out of the old, leave the door shut! Be prayerful not to allow the same silly rabbit to come back with new tricks. Do not compromise. Stand firm. Open up to receive every good deed God has in store for you. Be willing to except the people and the help God sends you. You are worthy. You are beautiful. You are loved by Jesus. How do I know? He sent His only Son to die in your place. Now that is love!

CLARITY QUESTIONS

1. Not based on what you have heard people say about you, describe the inner you in your words, in a paragraph.
2. What is one thing your spouse desires you to change or adjust?
   a. What is keeping you from making the requested changes?
3. Are you seeking a relationship to heal the pain of your last relationship?

Personal reflections

CHAPTER 10

Guard your heart

CHAPTER 10

Guard your heart

After I moved, a couple of my "friends" stopped coming around, because they couldn't stand to see me blessed after all I'd gone through. That brings to mind a well-known minister who was saddened by the jealousy of his "friends" A bishop friend of his laughed as he was sharing his disappointment with friends, who then asked him, "Would you prefer the blessings of God or those friends?" I'll answer it for him: *the blessings!* After paying the price, make up your mind to get all God has for you in spite of the opinions of family, friends, and foes. It's true that you may have to walk alone for a season or seasons, but when you get where you're going, people will be waiting to embrace and help you grow, so don't let anything stop you from going!

God is still restoring. The best is yet to come or be told. If you can, choose to see your friends blessed, even while you're still in need. Please stop, take a moment and celebrate their good fortune. Too many times when people have been on the mountain top, so to speak; now they are in the valley, and it's difficult for them to rejoice with people who are now on their mountain top experience. Remember, seasons do change. Whichever position you are in now, treat people with kindness, love and have compassion.

December 2017, would be my first Christmas divorced and without Mom. During that time, I realized that we must be mindful not to be insensitive to the needs of others. Colossians 4:6 NIV tells us "Let your conversation be gracious and attractive so that you will have the right response for everyone." It was close to Christmas when I was sharing my heart and the fact that we were divorced with someone I'd known for several years, who I'll call Tiffani. I was surprised when she asked, "Didn't you see it coming?" From her tone, I perceived she was asking why I had allowed it to happen. It was as if she had asked a physically abused woman, what she had done to make him hit her—that she must have done something to deserve it. Clearly, some people have little compassion unless it hits close to home. Not surprisingly, I was hoping to go and spend Christmas with people whose company I would enjoy. She had invited me a couple of times on other occasions, so I called to see if she had plans for Christmas. Of course, that was before our conversation. When she said she was having guests and then going out later, I asked if it was all right if I came by. She didn't come out and say no, but she had to abruptly end the call and said she'd call me back; she was shampooing her hair. She never did.

I was shocked by dear friends who put distance between us once I was divorced. I had no idea they would abandon me. I had to wonder why someone hadn't mentioned this issue before. When I asked other divorcees and widows, they agreed that such behavior was the norm. I had to wonder if we who are Believers, Spirit-filled, teaching and preaching—are really that insecure that single women would be a threat to us. And while I was looking for love and support, the only love I found was from the greatest love of all—the Lord Jesus. The truth is that everything that flows from our heart will show up in our actions. If your heart is not secure, it will show up in the way you treat people. Two months after my dear mom passed and one month after my necessary move, it was a tough pill to swallow that my friends weren't even calling to merely say hello or happy Thanksgiving, How are you feeling?

In the end, I was feeling that I had lost years, investing in a man who eventually decided to return to his vomit. Proverbs 26:11 NIV says: "As a dog returns to its vomit, so a fool repeats his foolishness." I must keep this in my heart: Nothing good is ever lost when we obey God, *nothing!* I know God is going to redeem the time, in Jesus' name. Even as I write this book, He has been restoring in many areas of my life.

Ladies, you don't have time to waste on a man who has no plan, no vision, and no direction for his life. I once read this memorable statement: "A man without a plan ends up living in his past." That is so true! If he doesn't know where he's going, how can he lead you? How can you be a helpmate for someone who has no direction— no goals—no endgame? And because God made woman to be a helpmeet to man, you will become frustrated, and feeling stagnated, with nowhere to go.

Perhaps you have your wedding dress all paid for, your invitations are in the mail, you selected a five star menu, Chiavari chairs are set to be delivered, with fine linen pressed and uniquely folded, but you know deep down in your heart--that you're making a major mistake. But, a major mistake can be avoided if you haven't made it yet.

Are you willing to take a chance, risking your health, your state of mind, your finances, and possibly your children's mental states? Did you know there are women who knowingly married the wrong man, and divorced six, seven, or even ten years later, and to this day, they can talk about nothing but how they were wronged by their ex-husbands.

Your heart is precious, you must be sober minded, realistic, the relationship must make sense before you open your heart to this person. Don't fool yourself, establishing his credit, connecting his life, making an investment into a man that's not even yours to begin with in the end can leave you deeply disappointed. By nature females are nurturers. But it's not for you to nurture every drive by that rolls your way. If you are the only one merely giving in the relationship, I must ask, is it a relationship? When are you going to allow a man to sow into you, to give to you?

When a true gentleman requests you to meet him for dinner, and he sincerely desires to pay for your gas, but you say no, because you feel that's being independent.

Therefore, each time he offers a kind gesture you simply say no. Sis, a leading man possesses the genuine desire to feel needed as well. Don't leave me now, stay with me; you have fixed his credit, supported him in getting his life together, but you want to remain independent. In the end, he takes his good credit and all that you have sown into him, goes and find a lady that allows him to feel needed. Girlfriend, we must counteract this. Can you see where we must be balanced in relationships?

I've heard women say God made me to be like this. But I would say: No, God created us in His image, but our decisions and experiences, if permitted will change us through pain, disappointment and bitterness, that has shaped and molded our life and jaded your outlook. But you don't have to stay there. If you're willing, He'll transform you and make your thoughts brand new, with great new potential that will lead you to your destiny.

Until a woman discovers her worth--exactly who God created her to be, and the power she possesses, she will settle for what she thinks she deserves or less, attributing it to God, when it's not at all what He had in mind for her.

I never will forget years ago when I met a young woman, (for the sake of privacy I'll call her Sylena.) It wasn't long before I discovered that Sylena wanted to be married, but I had no idea that she was desperate for a husband. She'd received a prophetic word about marriage. In fact, I dreamed that she was driving a new black Mercedes. She met a man and paid for him in more ways than one. It cost her big time. But the next time I saw her she had a cast on her arm, and her personality had begun to radically change. At that time, she was working at a company where she handled the finances, and she purchased the Mercedes after she met this man. In a phone conversation, she said to me, "You said you dreamed that I was in a black Mercedes." It's interesting how, as I write this book thoughts start to rush my mind. I now remember her as a person who tried to buy and control her friends with money. Once my late Pastor Jacqueline Lofton who was my dear friend, and I met Sylena for lunch. Pastor Jacqueline was an awesome woman of God. At lunch Sylena tried offering her nice things. My friend later she said she was trying to buy her, and her anointing was not for sale; she could not be purchased. She then moved forward in her relationship with this man. Not long afterward she purchased a beautiful new home; I even attended her housewarming. Then I went to her elaborate wedding. I assumed the money was part of her inheritance according to past conversations. One day God said to talk with her and warn her that if she listened to Him, He would turn things around for her. The day we spoke, I knew nothing of her illegal activity or that she was being investigated but she did mention that her company had called for an audit. During our phone conversation, she spoke softly and ended our call prematurely. As I was instructed, I met with her one morning and warned her. She seemed receptive as we parted ways. As I entered the door to my house, the phone was ringing—she was calling. She had talked with a couple of people from the church she attended, including a deacon, who said God wouldn't have warned her as I had said, because He only operates out of love, never judgment. After that time, we didn't speak for two years. Proverbs 16:16 reads: Pride goes before a disaster, and an arrogant attitude precedes a fall.

At that point, I had a phone call from a client I hadn't spoken with in a long time. During our conversation she casually mentioned that Sylena was in jail for embezzling money from her employer. She thought for sure I was aware of this news. Apparently, the police showed up at her home early one morning to arrest her, while her husband later turned state's evidence. The authorities took the house, the money, the Mercedes and everything else of value. I couldn't believe it! My heart went out to her. Over the next few days, I called to discover where she was being held, and went to see her, after learning that she'd been there over a year. Inmates don't know the identity of their visitors until they reach the visiting area, so she seemed a little surprised to see me, but not overjoyed. During our visit, I wept over her situation, but she appeared to either have peace or be resigned to her fate. We spoke that day and one other time, but she didn't seem excited about our visits, and told me her child might be coming to see her on the day I had planned to visit, so I never went back. Eventually, the penal system moved her out of state. I did however, continue to follow her tragic story for a season. I asked of God to cover and protect her. I wished her the best, both spiritually and naturally.

Sometime later, I went to get my nails manicured and was awaiting my technicians arrival when I ran into a young lady, I'll call Natasha, whom I hadn't seen for a while, but did not know that well. She began to talk about how she was doing after her divorce, and suffering abuse at his hand. As it turned out, she'd been married to the man Sylena later married. She added that Sylena had been warned not to get involved with him because he was abusive. As I always say, it's a small world, your name will go places you have never been.

Regarding her own situation, Natasha said, "God told me not to marry Steve, but I married him anyway." In the end, she had to flee to escape his ongoing abuse that ultimately affected her physically, verbally, mentally and financially, and even impacted her children. Including attorney fees, she has already spent over $70,000 to settle the divorce, and it wasn't over at that time . They had only the clothes on their backs when she left with her kids. He manipulated the court system so that he got custody of their children, and refuses to let her see them. His charismatic personality makes it easy to manipulate court employees assigned to their case. He cares nothing about the children, or even supervising their activities, which means they're allowed to stay up all night playing video games and missing school. As a result, these bright children are failing in school. As you can imagine, the children have no problem with their father's decisions, because they're getting exactly what they want. The mom is concerned about their education and asked the courts to transfer them back to their previous school, which is more demanding. The court agreed, but one son promised he'd never speak to her again if she forced the issue.

Natasha & Steve divorced more than ten years ago and she's still fighting this battle, spending money on attorneys all these years later. At this point, she might want to step back and ask God, "Should I fight in the natural and continue to spend money, or should I step back and allow you to fight this battle in order to get the victory and allow me to save money I can't spare?" Prayer is powerful weapon. In Ephesians 6:12 NIV we read: "For our struggle is not against flesh and blood, but against the rulers, against the authorities, against the powers of this dark world and against the spiritual forces of evil in the heavenly realms." Her battle is not against flesh and blood.

It's important not to *fall* in love, but to wisely choose to love and be loved. To fall in love is to be irresponsible, but to make a choice to love after consulting an all-knowing God, is to love responsibly. Keep in mind that He created the heavens and the earth, so He's pretty wise.

Ladies, it's just not worth it to say you have a man to keep from growing old alone. You can do badly all by yourself. But then, that would be your choice. It's hard to believe in this day and time, women in their late twenties feel old. I look at them side-eyed when they mention they feel old and are dreading going into their thirties!

Seek to have a covenant marriage. If you don't know what a covenant marriage is, learn. Wait for a man who loves God's presence and can't live without it. Genesis

2:15 NIV says this: "The Lord God took the man and put him in the Garden of Eden to work it and take care of it." So, ladies, the first thing God called man to do was *work*. He needs a job before he gets into a relationship in order to support his family. Your relationship is completely out of God's order if you are assuming the role of Adam while he is fulfilling the role of Eve because you don't want to live alone.

God designed man to be a leader who is full of vision. Woman was made to be his helpmate.

That's why mothers must be very mindful when raising boys into men. You don't want to mold your son into a lazy taker, who sits at home playing video games all day. That kind of enabling sends the wrong message to your son, who will then expect his working wife to support him, instead of taking the leadership to earn a living. To a hard-working man, God will then bring a loving wife who will then take her place as a great helpmate. In Genesis 2:15 Adam was put to work. In verse 18 The Lord God said, "It is not good for the man to be alone. I will make a helper suitable for him." Chapter 2:18-19 It goes on to say, "that God gave Adam the vision to name all living things. Now the Lord God had formed out of the ground, all the wild animals and all the birds in the sky. He brought them to the man to see what he would name them; and whatever the man called each living creature, that was its name. So the man gave names to all the livestock, the birds in the sky and all the wild animals."

Ladies, it was not until man was established with a job and vision that God gave him a wife. Genesis 2: 21-22 tells us: "So the Lord God caused the man to fall into a deep sleep; and while he was sleeping, he took one of the man's ribs and then closed up the place with flesh. Then the Lord God made a woman from the rib he had taken out of the man, and he brought her to the man."

Did you read that, ladies? God waited until man was established, before He gave him a wife. My point here is this: Stop wasting time on men who have no intention of working or getting married. If you play around with men with no vision, who are lustful and lazy, you'll miss out on the man God has for you. And believe me, when I say that He does have someone perfectly suited for you. All you have to do is get into your position— prepare. Strongly consider attending Christian singles classes. Imagine the awakening you would undoubtedly experience by sitting in on married couples conferences. Sis, you would obtain real-life wisdom and necessary knowledge. The key word here is PREPARATION.

That brings me to another important point. If you are married, try not to complain regarding your husband working too many long hours, instead talk to him about making quality time for you. Either you want him to do what God created him to do, or you want a lustful, lazy man with no vision. What is a lustful man? He is someone who doesn't want to work or marry, just wants to have sex without commitment. He has no desire for a covenant marriage relationship.

If you have divorced and are still emotionally tied to that person, or perhaps the person you love is married to someone else, I strongly suggest you move away from that circumstance and go to God in prayer. God is not going to give you a married man, that is adultery. He is not going to commit sin against himself. Become very uncomfortable and cry out to God until that yearning breaks off of you. There is a price to pay when you give your body to someone who is not your husband, even if it's only in your head and heart. Spend time with God and ask Him to do spiritual surgery on your emotions until it manifests on the outside. Ask God to direct you to a Christian counselor for a season. There's nothing like a good Spirit-filled counselor who hears the voice of God as it pertains to your situation. But whatever you do, start the journey to healing and change, so you can position yourself for *happiness*. "Happiness Is an Inside Job."

Love yourself enough to be faithful, to wait on a healthy, happy marriage. Refuse to fall for the first man who pays attention to you. Step back, pray, take it slow, and ask questions. Don't lose everything you've invested in your spiritual walk, to satisfy your sexual desires and turn your back on God. After all, He loves you more than anyone else ever could. Don't hurt the one Person who will never abandon you. He is a rewarder of those who diligently seek Him and walk uprightly. He will reward you in ways you cannot imagine if you continue to live *holy*. Choose to be happy while you wait. Do not wait on a relationship to make you happy. Remember that happiness is an inside job." You don't have to wait to begin fulfilling your own happiness. Ladies put off traveling, trying something new until they get married. Why? Don't allow precious time to past you buy.

After I asked God if I should marry my then-fiancé, I made the decision to trust whatever God said. It was a conscious decision to keep my marriage vows before God—a matter of choice. I chose to stand and honor God in my covenant marriage through good, not so good, bad, hurtful, disappointing days and even what seemed like endless years. Divorce was not an option for me. Was it easy? No, there were many days, which would have been unbearable if God had not carried and covered me through the process. There were days I wanted to file for divorce, but I hung in there and allowed God to guide me. Eventually the time came when God would no longer sit on the throne and hold His peace regarding my situation. God loved me and was obligated to me, just as He is obligated to anyone who belongs to Him and does things His way, not on their terms.

You have my love and support in moving forward and winning in life and your goals, know that I am praying for you. You are more than enough!

I sincerely pray the words in this book have been impactful! To my single ladies wait on your King, be prepared when he is presented. As for my married Queens, I pray you receive the strength required as your marriage is transformed into what God predestined, days and nights filled with love, forgiveness and joy.

What did you receive from the clarity questions? Look at your answers truthfully. Pray over your answers and seek God to steer you where you're falling short.

You do not have to be alone or lonely. If you would like to join us being happy and traveling, join our travel club, live life and travel on purpose, unapologetically. Get your passport, pack your suitcase and let the wind of the Holy Spirit guide us. Email us at: Eventsbyarlisia@ gmail.com In the subject put: Happiness Is An Inside Job/ Travel.

Finally, words have power, I would like to make a declaration over your life. Words can bring death or life! Talk too much, and you will eat everything you say. Proverbs 18:21 This is one time we want to eat our every word and reap the results.

DECLARATION
(READ OUT LOUD)

I speak to every broken place in my life and command healing and wholeness to come. I shall never be deceived by the plans and plots of the enemy again. I decree and declare that my discernment is increasing every day. I decree that I am rising up in courage and strength, to be who God called me to be when I was formed in your mother's womb. I am wise; I walk in God's strength; I am more than enough. I shall succeed in every area of life. The man after God's heart, the man who desires to be my husband shall pursue me, love me, cherish and protect me, cover me, as I do the same for him till death do we part.

DECLARATION FOR MARRIED LADIES:

I decree that myself and my husband walk in peace and love abides on the inside. I pray for humility to overtake and conquer us. I silence the negative voices from outsiders, their words have no effect over us. I destroy the power and influence of their words. I pray for a revival to take place in your life and marriage. I pray for the restoration of love and trust. I cover us in the blood of Jesus.

Rise up, pray and follow the instructions of the Holy Spirit. In Jesus' name, Amen. I love and believe in you.

XOXO,
Arlisia Staley

310-402 9093

Made in the USA
Monee, IL
28 September 2020

43473150R10122